P9-CLC-272

Just-Right Comprehension Mini-Lessons

GRADES 2-3

CHERYL M. SIGMON

New York • Toronto • London • Auckland • Sydney
Mexico City • New Delhi • Hong Kong • Buenos Aires

Teaching *Resources*

Dedication

In memory of my mother, Wakefield Baltzegar Mahaffey, whose life on earth ended during the writing of this book. As a kind, selfless woman of tremendous faith, she was the greatest teacher in my life and will remain a lasting inspiration.
—CMS

Acknowledgments

As always, I owe a debt of gratitude to my editor, Merryl Maleska Wilbur. Thank you for your patience and your guidance—especially through the trials and tribulations of this book. As always, in so many ways your talent has helped to make this book a useful tool for classroom teachers. What a pleasure and privilege to work with you!

A special thanks to Virginia Dooley, Terry Cooper, and my other Scholastic family—for your faith in this new series and for your compassion during the writing of this book.

Lisa D. Gilpin, Teacher and consultant, Versailles, IN

Sylvia M. Ford, Consultant, Columbia, SC

Marian S. Hodge, Consultant, Savannah, GA

Alberta Porter, Sandra Lloyd, and the teachers, special educators, reading specialists, and administrators of Magnolia Elementary School, Joppa, MD

Administrators and teachers of Sand Creek Elementary School, North Vernon, IN

Dr. Linda Walker, and the teachers and administrators of Montpelier Elementary, Northside Elementary, and Southside Elementary in the Blackford County School District, Hartford City, IN

Dr. Libby Hostetler, Principal, Kaye Phillips and the teachers of Bluffton Elementary School, Bluffton, OH

Sierra Jackson, Principal, and the teachers of Custer Hill Elementary School, Ft. Riley, KS

Gloria Quattrone, Principal, and Jennifer Hyde, Jennifer Workman, Deena Fuller for their pictures and ideas, and all primary teachers of Southlawn Elementary School, Liberal, KS

Lana Evans, Director of Curriculum, and the principals and teachers of USD 480, Liberal, KS

Lisa Wiedmann and the teachers of the Rhinelander School System, Rhinelander, WI

Becky McCrary, Clear Creek Elementary, Hendersonville, NC

Beyond the research that has been cited in this book, gratitude is extended to the teachers who took that research and made it practical and teachable in the classroom. Stephanie Harvey and Ann Goudvis in *Strategies that Work*; Deb Miller's *Reading with Meaning*; Ellin Keene and Susan Zimmerman's *Mosaic of Thought*; and Linda Hoyt's *Reread, Revise, and Revisit*—all give us not only the insight but also the courage to begin our own exploration in the classroom without fearing the unknown.

Cover design and cover photo by Maria Lilja.
Interior design by Holly Grundon.
Interior photos courtesy of the author.

ISBN-13: 978-0-439-89905-5
ISBN-10: 0-439-89905-2
Copyright © 2007 by Cheryl M. Sigmon.
All rights reserved.
Printed in the U.S.A.

1 2 3 4 5 6 7 8 9 10   40   15 14 13 12 11 10 09 08 07

Table *of* Contents

Introduction

The focus of this book, reading comprehension, has for several decades been considered the "essence of reading" (Durkin, 1993). Many of us have sat alongside a child who can, with great precision, "call" all the words on a page correctly. However, this same child is clearly lost when asked to talk about the content he or she has just read. Not only do we now know that good word callers are not really reading but we have changed our instruction accordingly.

Some of the greatest influence on reading instruction stems from the research into metacognition and constructivist reading in the early 1970s. This research shifted the emphasis in reading from the word and sentence level of text to the reader as thinker and meaning-maker, with the interaction between reader and text assuming central importance (Bransford, Barclay, and Franks, 1972). Subsequent research comparing normal and low-achieving readers to high achievers revealed a marked difference in the most successful readers' ability to engage in metacognitive thinking during reading (Palincsar and Brown, cited in Johnston and Winograd, 1985). Metacognition has been defined as "having knowledge (cognition) and having understanding, control over and appropriate use of that knowledge" (Tei and Stewart, 1985). Perhaps more succinctly defined as the ability to think about one's own thinking, metacognition involves such activities as a reader's purposefully planning before reading, making and confirming predictions, and self-monitoring understanding.

Reading instruction now has at its center the goal of helping students develop good habits—constructing meaning, interacting with text metacognitively, and reading with genuine fluency. In line with that goal, this book aims to help teachers put solid research into practice through simple but powerful daily mini-lessons. The hope is that these mini-lessons can offer students tools and ways of approaching text that turn into lifelong lessons to be applied far beyond the classroom.

CONTEXTS AND FRAMEWORKS FOR THESE MINI-LESSONS

These mini-lessons are the teacher's opportunity to provide direct instruction in key comprehension skills and strategies that first graders need to become good readers. The lessons' great advantage is that they can be implemented in a number of different natural classroom contexts. For example, these mini-lessons will work well within guided reading lessons; reading workshops; tutorial sessions; small-group instruction; and content area lessons, in which understanding about how to read and manage text is important. Here's a brief description of how they might work within each of these contexts:

- **Guided Reading Lessons** The first segment of a guided reading lesson—the time dedicated to a teacher's modeling what students are expected to do during their own reading—is an ideal instructional home for these mini-lessons. Frequently there is also a step in the mini-lesson outline that describes students' own reading and sometimes one that involves the teacher's closure and summarizing. Thus, in several different ways, you should be able to fold these lessons right into the framework of a guided reading lesson.

- **Reading Workshops** The Reading Workshop begins with a teacher's modeling and demonstrating what a good reader does. These mini-lessons are an ideal launch point for the Workshop because direct instruction and modeling lie at the core of the lessons.

- **Tutorial Sessions** These lessons are ideal for use in tutorial sessions that target specific students' needs. Just use the book's table of contents and the Matrix of Standards to locate a lesson that focuses on a particular skill or strategy needed by a student. Also, because the mini-lessons are written step-by-step in a clearly delineated standard format, they should be accessible to all, including assistants supporting regular classroom teachers.

- **Small-Group Instruction** Just as with Tutorial Sessions, these mini-lessons can drastically cut planning time for teachers who need to design lessons for targeted small-group instruction. Identify the common instructional needs of several students and then use the table of contents and the Matrix of Standards to locate the appropriate lesson(s) to teach that skill or strategy.

- **Content Area Lessons** Many of these mini-lessons make use of science or social studies text, thus demonstrating how easy it is to integrate literacy and content instruction. Students need to see how they can use literacy skills to help them make sense of content area information and communicate it to others.

How These Mini-Lessons Are Specific for Grades 2–3 Curriculum

Comprehension lessons at the second- and third-grade level share a number of fundamental similarities with those at the first-grade level. Instruction still needs to address different learning modalities—visual, auditory, kinesthetic, and tactile—and should thus include many hands-on possibilities, such as work with sticky notes, graphic organizers, and highlighters. Think-aloud modeling in which teachers demonstrate metacognitive and other mental processes involved in reading is still at the core of instruction. And, of course, since transfer is the ultimate goal of all comprehension instruction, second- and third-grade teachers should continue to encourage transfer of students' learning to other areas.

Beyond these similarities, however, there are significant differences between instructional expectations for first graders and those for second and third graders. These differences are reflected in the mini-lessons you'll find in this book as compared to the first book in the series.

By second and third grade, students usually have developed a good understanding of basic print and language concepts. Now they are ready to benefit from instruction in fluency development and in more sophisticated decoding strategies. Thus, the first section of this book has a different focus from the opening section in the first-grade book. Here, rather than basic concepts, the first section includes lessons that emphasize reading with fluency, high-frequency words, and useful decoding strategies. The aim of these lessons is to help lay the groundwork for all subsequent sections, which address the skills and strategies necessary for reading comprehension in second and third grade.

In several other important ways, second and third graders are ready for greater challenges than first graders. In their early lives at home and in kindergarten and first grade, most children are exposed to a good deal of narrative text. They become familiar with story structure and framework such as beginning, middle, and end and with story elements like character, setting, and plot. At second and third grade, narrative text continues to be important but instruction can now target more complex reading behaviors. For example, students are ready to analyze literary elements rather than simply to identify them.

Even more significantly, the focus shifts from an emphasis on narrative text to one that increasingly emphasizes informational text. Because the second- and third-grade curriculum includes a good deal of content area study, many of these mini-lessons ask students to work with content textbooks and informational reading selections. With direct instruction and teachers' assistance, second and third graders can handle expository text internal and external structure. These lessons will help develop their confidence.

By second and third grade, students are expected to handle tasks like analyzing literary elements and navigating expository text structure.

On an overall basis, we expect students at the second- and third-grade level to become increasingly more strategic in their approach to a wide variety of text. Thus, along with narrative and informational text, a number of these mini-lessons highlight poetry and drama. And, whatever their content focus, all the mini-lessons at these grade levels provide students greater independence and more frequent opportunities for critical and creative thinking.

Standards

Along with the National Standards, the standards of the following 11 states were gathered to create the curriculum for this book: California, Colorado, Florida, Indiana, Missouri, New York, Pennsylvania, South Carolina, Texas, Virginia, and Washington.

HOW THESE MINI-LESSONS WERE DEVELOPED

The curriculum for the lessons in this book is based on a number of documents. As a first step in developing the lessons, I looked into whether educators around the United States generally hold common beliefs about what students need to know and do in first-grade reading comprehension. I selected eleven states that represent different geographical regions as well as diverse populations and studied the standards documents for these states. Not surprisingly, I found a high correlation of commonalities among the documents. Some terminology differed, but the basic thinking was similar. Across the country, it seems that we have pretty much agreed about what constitutes good reading among our first graders.

Next, I studied another important and widely regarded document, *The National Reading Panel Report* (2000), to find out how its experts regard reading comprehension and whether its beliefs are congruent with the states' beliefs. I discovered that while the standards/objectives defined by the states were more discrete and specific than the broader strategies identified in the national document, the two sources corroborated each other and were highly compatible.

Indeed, the two sources work hand-in-hand extremely well. The states' standards can be seen as the focused guidelines necessary to help students achieve the broader, more general strategies suggested by the National Reading Panel. Therefore, in organizing this book and developing the lessons, I used the national strategies as the basis for the section divisions and the more discrete standards as the springboards for the lessons themselves.

THE NATURE OF A GOOD MINI-LESSON

An effective reading comprehension mini-lesson is direct and explicit and focused solely on the targeted comprehension skill or strategy. Lessons shouldn't confuse the students by introducing grammar, mechanics, usage, long and short vowel sounds, digraphs, and similar skills. There are other opportunities in the instructional day when these skills can best be taught and understood. Reserve your mini-lesson exclusively for those skills and strategies that have direct impact on the meaning derived from reading text.

There is another key aspect to the effective mini-lesson: While direct and explicit, mini-lesson instruction does not simply tell students what they need to know. Instead, it involves a teacher's active, dynamic modeling of the targeted skill and/or strategy. Modeling the thinking and the decisions that a reader must make, even the little ones, will allow these same thought processes to become

An effective mini-lesson usually starts with a teacher's modeling. In this lesson a teacher thinks aloud about a book she is reading to the class.

part of your students' habits. Thus, a critical part of your modeling is "thinking aloud," or expressing aloud the process you are following as you read a piece of text and apply a strategy or utilize a skill. Many students, especially beginning readers, don't know how to actively reflect as they read. Your demonstrating how to do this becomes a key part of your students' development as readers.

PEEKING IN ON TWO TEACHERS

Here are two mini-lessons that show a clear difference in their approach to instruction. Let's peek into the classrooms below to compare the effectiveness of the two different lessons.

Teacher A

In her classroom, Teacher A gathers students together on the carpet near her rocking chair where she has placed an easel that holds a Big Book. She introduces the book through a quick picture walk to familiarize students with the contents. She then introduces some vocabulary that corresponds to illustrations and teaches the meaning of several related words not in the text. Next she explains to students how to identify the main character in a narrative text. Finally, she invites the students to read along with her as she reads the text. The students seem to enjoy the story. Teacher A concludes the lesson by asking a number of comprehension questions about the story, such as: "Who was the main character?"; "Where did the story take place?"; and "What did Harry say after the dog ran away?"

Teacher B

In his classroom, Teacher B begins a lesson by showing students a handful of seashells he brought back from his summer vacation and asking if any students have ever found shells on a trip to the beach. Then, he shows students the cover of the book the class will read today. He tells them the purpose of today's lesson—making predictions about a book based on the title, cover picture clues, and any other cover information. He explains that he is going to demonstrate the process he goes through himself when he picks up a new book and is not sure what it is about. He tells students, "When I read a book's title and see the pictures on the cover, my brain starts to tell me right away what the book might be about." He offers several ideas aloud, jots down these thoughts on a chart, and then invites students to suggest additional predictions. "Now, we'll read this book and find out if our predictions are right. If they're not, that's okay. We just have to remember to think this way when we read." The teacher reads the story aloud and then holds a brief discussion so that the class can talk about the initial predictions.

At the closure of a well-constructed lesson, you'll likely find students better prepared to answer a most important question. Read on to find out exactly what the question is.

DID THE LESSON SUCCEED?

A great aid to teachers in analyzing the success of reading lessons is asking the simple question: *What did my students learn today that will make them better readers?* And you can make this question even more powerful by asking it directly of students themselves. You may be surprised to hear what your students have to say! Often when we think we're communicating something, it's heard in an entirely different way—especially in dealing with first graders.

If, in answer to this question, students begin to retell the story, they have probably not grown much as readers from the lesson. The students in Teacher A's classroom would be more likely to retell the story. The lesson has several basic shortcomings: It doesn't give students a real reason to care about or even grasp the main purpose of the lesson; it doesn't stay focused on the skill at hand; it doesn't actively demonstrate how the reading skill is to be applied; it doesn't engage students in the process; and it doesn't close in a way that summarizes their learning. In Teacher B's classroom, on the other hand, each of these instructional elements does take place. These students would most likely be able to say in their own words that they've learned about making predictions and why it is important to a good reader. And if they're able to articulate what they have learned about the skill or strategy, then there's a greater likelihood that they'll take that skill and use it when it counts—in their real reading!

HOW TO USE THIS BOOK

INSTRUCTIONAL FLEXIBILITY

If your school uses a basal reader program for instruction, there are several ways to organize your year using the lessons in this book. You might follow your basal curriculum and consult the table of contents in this book to find a lesson to help you teach the skill/strategy the basal curriculum calls for. Or, you might follow this book, and then use your basal as it meets the text criteria specified for each lesson.

If your school's approach is literature based, you can follow your local curriculum and consult the table of contents in this book to see which lesson correlates with the defined skill/strategy. Or, you can follow this book and use your literature for the context of the lessons, again using the text specifications provided in each lesson to locate appropriate material. You might also choose to use available content texts, including textbooks, so that students will become comfortable with expository text.

No matter how you use this book within your overall reading instruction, it's important to take your local or state curriculum and cross-check it with the table of contents to see if any gaps exist.

You'll also be the best person to make the decision about how often a skill or strategy needs to be revisited and reinforced.

SEQUENCING YOUR LESSONS

For the most part, you can pick and choose lessons randomly throughout the book. We recommend viewing the sections as a menu. You can select lessons appropriately based on your students' needs and on opportunities to integrate lessons with other content being taught.

There are just a few exceptions to this recommendation. First, because Section One deals with basic word-level concepts, its lessons should be included at the beginning of the school year and reinforced until students are comfortable with the basics. Then you'll be ready to branch out far beyond the foundational concepts of these lessons.

The other exception is those lessons that are set up purposely in a certain sequence. These are clearly identified as having multiple parts from the start. It's best to look out ahead of time for these lessons so that you won't wind up getting the cart before the horse with activities or with presentation of concepts.

ADDITIONAL CONSIDERATIONS

There are a few additional key considerations to keep in mind as you approach these lessons and as you consider the best ways you will use them within your overall reading curriculum. Below is a list of some of these considerations:

- What printed text should be used? Many of these lessons suggest specific titles but also provide general guidelines to allow you the freedom to choose what you want to use and to take into consideration the materials that are available in your own teaching situation.

- Is there any vocabulary essential to understanding the printed text you'll be using for a given lesson? You'll want to keep the presentation of vocabulary to a minimum within the context of these mini-lessons, but some words may be critical to preview for students.

- How much support will students need to read the text for a given lesson? Even if a lesson suggests reading the text aloud to your class, you are definitely the best person to decide if a different presentation is called for. Perhaps, for certain lessons and in certain situations, you'll want your students to read chorally with you or with a partner or a small group.

- What will tomorrow's lesson be? You'll base this on the closure from the day's lesson and on feedback from previous lessons. If at the conclusion of a lesson you see that your students "got it" and don't need any clarification, then perhaps you'll choose to focus on another skill or strategy the following day. Or perhaps you'll feel they need a little more—or occasionally a lot more—practice, in which case you'll continue to teach and reteach the current skill or strategy. It's all based on students' needs and the evidence you're able to gather.

Just-Right Comprehension Mini-Lessons: Grades 2–3

- The final point is perhaps the most obvious, but it's too often overlooked in the face of all the other demands confronting teachers, so we feel it's worth underscoring. As you plan each lesson, it's clarifying to ask one simple question of yourself: *What do I need to teach that will help my students become better readers?* A direct answer to that question alone would eliminate many lessons presently taught in our classrooms. Too often we teach lessons that are ends in themselves. The text isn't what it's about at all—it's really about how to read the text. What we need to teach are lessons that become the means to achieve more long-range goals for our students as readers. It is the hope and intent of this book to meet that need.

CONSTRUCTING TOOL KITS

Have you noticed some students in your classroom who can sit quietly, perhaps squirming just a bit, for the full duration of a read-aloud? Surely, you've noticed those others—the ones who tend to be always in motion. They drum their fingers on the desk, chew their pencils, shake their legs, or twist and turn in their seats. These kinesthetic learners actually need to move to learn.

Every classroom includes students at both ends of this spectrum, as well as those in the middle. The lessons in this book promote instruction that taps the different learning styles of all students. You'll find that most lessons offer students the opportunity to be not only mentally engaged in reading but physically/tactilely engaged as well. Something as simple as having students place sticky notes on certain pages or moving a "magic" reading stick across the page can help focus energy and attention. So we've structured these lessons to include a great deal of students' active involvement. Even those students who don't need this extra element to remain engaged in learning can benefit from and enjoy this kind of dynamic interaction with text.

To make these kinds of activities manageable in the classroom, you may want to create simple kits to help maximize the time your students have to devote to their tasks. Your students will love having their very own tool kits, and you'll love seeing how engaged they become as they put the kits to use. To construct the kits, you'll first need a sealable sandwich bag for each student in the classroom. You can easily personalize these bags by printing your students' names on self-adhesive mailing labels and sticking them to the bags. See the example above.

The tools should be introduced gradually so that students are taught the appropriate use of each and so that the tools won't be overwhelming to them in the beginning. Here are some tools that you might choose to include in your students' kits:

- **Sticky Notes** About 12 on a pad per kit will be sufficient for a few lessons.

- **VIP Strips** These are sticky notes that you pre-cut, snipping several times toward the sticky end to form "fingers" that students can tear off as needed to mark text. "VIP" stands for Very Important Points (Hoyt, 1999).

- **Magic Reading Sticks** These are ice-pop sticks or tongue depressors with tips dipped in glue and then in a pretty glitter. Each student needs only one of these for—among many possible uses—tracking print, identifying vocabulary words, and underscoring text clues.

- **Sticky Sticks** These come in packs and look similar to pipe cleaners but have a waxy coating that adheres to book pages. They can cling to a book page and then be stripped away without leaving a residue. They are malleable and also can be cut into smaller strips. They are used to highlight and identify words, phrases, and clues.

- **Pocket Chart Highlighters** These are brightly colored, transparent, flexible plastic strips, approximately 2 inches by 4 inches. They come in packs of about 24 and are useful for highlighting sections of text.

- **Highlighter Pens** These come in a variety of colors and are used to highlight text.

- **Bookmarks** These can be handy as placeholders and can serve double duty to track print or highlight sentences that are discussed. Bookmarks can be purchased, downloaded free from the Internet, or made by students.

- **Response Cards** These are useful in eliciting responses from all students, thereby helping circumvent the frequent classroom phenomenon in which a few students always respond while others remain passive. Each student's tool kit contains one index card with the word *Yes* and another with the word *No*. When you ask a question, all students are to respond with one of the cards.

- **Crayons** A crayon or two can be included for use as highlighters to mark text and for occasional additional uses.

- **Word Frame** For this, you'll use a die-cut template to cut an appealing shape from construction paper. After the figure is cut, snip a small window in the figure. (You might need to fold the figure to make an evenly cut window.) Then, run the figure through your laminator and trim the edges. The result is a fun figure with a window for students to frame words and phrases. See right for one example.

You may think of other items—such as paper clips and index cards to mark pages—to include in the kits as the year progresses. Have fun creating these kits and guiding your students to use them to get more hands-on involved in reading!

BEYOND THESE LESSONS

When asked why they're learning to read, many students respond that it's to please the teacher—which in one sense is an admirable answer, but not at all why they need to learn to read! They are also likely to respond that they're learning to read to pass to the next grade—again an ambitious goal, but not why we want them to learn to read. We must do two things in addition to teaching the skills and strategies in this book so that students will realize that reading is both a necessary and joyful part of daily life.

First, we must continue to show them the "real-world" purposes served by reading and being literate. That means bringing in real-world reading materials to share and making those available to the students—take-out menus, pet-care booklets, nutrition pamphlets, the school/district newsletter, how-to manuals, dental hygiene and health-care pamphlets, recipe books, newspapers, the school menu, thank-you notes from relatives and friends, postcards we've received, e-mail messages from teachers in other parts of the country, and so many other real-world types of written communication. Students need to see clearly that reading is necessary in our everyday lives.

Second, we need to read aloud to students every single day so that they discover the real joy of reading. You'll help them understand quickly that the squiggly lines on the page do, indeed, have meaning. Read to them often without any lessons connected—just for pure enjoyment. Let them hear the different sounds and patterns of language and the stories and information that will challenge their minds and imaginations.

Good Luck and Enjoy!

Inviting students to read real-world materials, like magazines, not only increases motivation but also helps students understand that reading is part of our everyday lives.

A lifelong love of reading often starts with sharing and discussing books with friends.

Matrix of Standards*

Standards	Lesson Page
Use a variety of strategies to derive meaning from texts	All lessons
Read widely from different genres and from classical and contemporary text	All lessons
Use content/specialized words	27, 42, 65, 95, 113, 114
Apply different meanings in different contexts	27
Identify and use synonyms, antonyms, homonyms, homophones, and homographs	27
Use basic elements of phonetic analysis (hear, segment, substitute, blend sounds, and recognize visual cues, onsets, and patterns) to read unfamiliar words in text	23, 24
Use print conventions to aid comprehension and to build fluency	20, 21, 22
Use structural cues/polysyllabic decoding strategies (including common prefixes, compound words, contractions) to decode and understand text	23, 24
Use context clues to construct meaning	23, 24, 36, 42, 50
Use syntax to construct meaning	23, 24, 36
Read aloud smoothly, easily, and expressively in familiar text (employing proper pacing, phrasing, intonation, rhythm, and rate)	20, 21, 22, 51
Know rhymes, rhythm, and patterned structures in children's texts, including poetry	20, 21, 22, 118
Know common sight words appropriate to grade level	25, 26
Self-monitor comprehension and use repair strategies	30, 31, 32, 33, 34, 35, 36, 38, 39, 49, 52, 55, 81, 82, 83, 84, 85, 86, 87
Self-correct using appropriate strategies and cueing systems	30, 31, 33, 34, 35, 36, 38, 39, 49
Find and/or recall significant details in text	33, 34, 38, 39, 45, 49, 54, 90, 92, 94, 95, 97, 98, 99, 117
Distinguish between fact and opinion	32
Reread to clarify	34, 35, 36
Explain what good readers do	30, 31, 33, 34, 35, 36, 38, 39
Select and read for extended periods of time to derive pleasure and to gain information	47, 49, 50, 51, 52
Establish purposes for reading (to be informed, to follow directions, to be entertained, to use environmental text)	107, 108
Ask and answer questions about texts before, during, and after reading	31, 42, 43, 44, 45, 46, 47, 49, 50, 51, 52, 53, 54, 55
Make predictions about texts	42, 43, 44, 45, 46, 47, 49, 50, 51, 52
Confirm predictions by identifying key words/signpost words	42, 43, 44, 45, 46
Respond to questions of *who, what, why, when, where*, and *how* and ask for clarification on unclear areas	53, 54, 55, 107, 108
Ask questions to guide topic selections	47, 49, 50, 51, 52
Make connections between texts read aloud or independently and prior knowledge, other texts, and the world	42, 81, 82, 83, 84, 85, 86, 87

Just-Right Comprehension Mini-Lessons: Grades 2–3

Read, listen to, and discuss a variety of literature representing different perspectives and generate a personal response	82, 83, 118
Respond to texts through a variety of methods, such as creative dramatics, writing, and graphic art in a variety of formats	64, 70, 72, 74, 81, 82, 83, 86, 94, 118
Develop vocabulary through concrete and/or meaningful experiences	27, 42, 58, 60, 61, 62, 64, 65, 70, 71, 74
Classify and categorize to organize information	58, 60, 61, 62, 64, 65, 78, 90, 92, 94, 95, 97, 98, 99
Identify internal structure of text: cause-and-effect relationships; listing; sequence; compare/contrast; problem/solution; beginning, middle, end	58, 60, 64, 102, 117
Create mental images when reading	69, 70, 71, 72, 73, 74, 76, 77, 78
Compose visual images from what is read	58, 60, 61, 62, 64, 74
Begin to identify devices of figurative language such as similes, metaphors, onomatopoeia, and alliteration to enhance understanding	77, 78
Begin to compare and contrast similarities and differences within a text and between two texts	61, 82, 83, 102
Draw conclusions and make inferences	87
Summarize main ideas, events, ideas, and themes in texts	53, 65, 90, 92, 94, 95, 97, 98, 99, 112, 113, 114, 115, 116
Explain steps/follow steps in a process	109
Identify the title, author, and illustrator of a text as well as parts of a book (cover, table of contents, title page)	102, 103, 104, 105
Identify sequence and logical order	60, 64, 109, 117
Identify beginning, middle, and end of a story	97, 98
Use graphic representations such as charts, graphs, pictures, and graphic organizers as information sources and as a means of organizing information and events logically	58, 60, 61, 62, 64, 65, 69, 70, 71, 72, 73, 74, 76, 77, 78, 109, 115
Practice test-like questions	107, 108
Identify characters, setting, problem, solution, speaker, theme, and plot in a literary work	38, 39, 60, 62, 72, 73, 99, 117
Analyze literary elements	39, 62, 72, 73, 99
Distinguish between fiction and nonfiction	102, 103, 110, 111, 112, 113, 114, 115, 116, 117
Identify the characteristics of genres such as fiction, poetry, drama, and informational texts	20, 21, 22, 38, 39, 44, 45, 46, 60, 62, 72, 73, 62, 98, 99, 102, 103, 109, 110, 111, 112, 113, 114, 115, 116, 118
Use simple reference materials to obtain information (tables of contents, books, dictionaries, software, chapter titles, guide words, indices)	44, 45, 46, 47, 98, 102, 103, 109, 110, 111, 112, 113, 114, 115, 116
Use text features to locate and understand information	107, 108, 109, 110, 111, 112, 113, 114, 115, 116
Identify elements of drama (playwright, theater, stage, act, dialogue, scene)	103
Identify how same topic is treated differently by various genres	118

*Along with the National Standards, the standards of the following 11 states were gathered to create the curriculum for this book: California, Colorado, Florida, Indiana, Missouri, New York, Pennsylvania, South Carolina, Texas, Virginia, and Washington.

Developing Basic Word Level and Fluency Skills

By second and third grade, most students have moved beyond the need for instruction in basic print and language concepts like understanding the characteristics of letters, words, sentences, and paragraphs. Instead, they are ready to concentrate on building fluency—to read at an appropriate rate with the correct intonation and phrasing, which will in turn help improve comprehension. In fact, fluency is now recognized as one of several critical factors necessary for reading comprehension (National Reading Panel Report; NICHHD, 2000).

The lessons in this section focus on fluency from several different perspectives—print mechanics, decoding skills, high-frequency word recognition, and familiarity with words that have multiple meanings. First, we ask students to pay closer attention to the mechanical clues on the page— commas, end punctuation, and lines—so that they can read with ease. Because we do this in the context of poetry and song lyrics, students get a chance to experience the real-life value of these text signals as well as to have some fun while learning.

The section also includes several lessons that focus on decoding unfamiliar words in text. It's important for students to know they have different options when they encounter unknown words. The lessons offer a number of quick and easy decoding strategies that support students as they read. One of these lessons provides students with a year-round tool, a special bookmark, which they can readily refer to during independent reading. The more familiar students are with a variety of decoding strategies, the easier it will be for them to read fluently, without losing the meaning of what they are reading.

Additionally, as part of their fluency development, students need a good deal of practice with high-frequency words—essential words that constitute the majority of text students encounter. Achieving automatic recognition of these words is fundamental to fluency and comprehension. Once they are able to instantly recognize these words, young readers no longer have to stop and deliberate about how to decode (or encode) them. Instead, they are free to concentrate on the more difficult aspects of reading and writing—comprehension and composition. For these reasons, we've included several lessons in this section that target high-frequency words.

Word knowledge is another fundamental building block for increasing fluency and comprehension. Thus, the final lesson helps students build their meaning vocabularies (and they get to play a riddle-like game at the same time!).

In fact, playing games and having fun is characteristic of this whole section. The lessons take what has frequently been taught in a dry, dull manner and engage students in active, even humorous participation. You'll find them sipping cocoa as they read in the spotlight of a Poetry Café or flyswatting words in competition with one another—and discovering fluency and decoding can be fun! So, let's get on with it!

This girl is building fluency as she uses a magic stick to stay focused on her reading.

This Word Wall supports students' developing fluency by displaying high-frequency words for class reference.

THREE-PART LESSON: POETRY CAFÉ

PART 1: ANALYZING TEXT FOR SIGNALS

Explanation

In this three-part lesson, students develop fluency while experiencing favorite song lyrics or poetry verses in a new way. As they focus on reading fluently, they're bound to freshly appreciate the poems and songs. In this first part, students learn to watch for text signals that can help them adjust their voices. The lesson culminates on the third day in a 1960s-style "coffeehouse" experience.

Skill Focus

Reading aloud with appropriate pacing, phrasing, intonation, rhythm, and rate; identifying rhymes, rhythm, and patterned structures in poetry

Materials & Resources

Text
- Popular or traditional songs and poems (Used in this three-part lesson: "The Erie Canal" from *Gonna Sing My Head Off!* collected by Kathleen Krull)

Other
- Transparency of the selected song or poem

Bonus Ideas

Set aside a spot in your classroom library for students' own collections of favorite songs and poems. (You might suggest that they use the Internet to locate favorites; it can be a great resource for finding appropriate lyrics. Be sure to let students know that you reserve the right to censor any lyrics that contain objectionable words or content!)

STEPS

1. Explain to students that in the 1960s poetry reached new audiences in cafes and coffeehouses. These coffeehouses invited poets, many of whom had not published their work, to read and recite their poetry. Tell the class that they will replicate this experience in this series of lessons.

2. Tell students that a critical aspect of all reading is achieving a fluent rhythm, pace, rate, phrasing, and tone. Point out that this is especially true of reading song lyrics and poems. You might share the following brief definitions of these important terms with students:
   - **Rhythm:** attention to stressed and unstressed syllables
   - **Pace and rate:** speed at which text is read
   - **Phrasing:** grouping words and pausing appropriately
   - **Tone:** expression based on purpose

3. Explain that printed text frequently provides clues about how readers should adjust their voices—both in silent and oral reading—appropriately. Research and/or brainstorm a list of different print signals that provide this information. You might allow students to thumb through various books to locate examples of these signals. On a transparency or the board, record the findings in two columns. One sample list is below.

4. Now display the transparency of the song you've selected. With students' input, highlight text signals. As you highlight each signal, note how it tells you to make your voice sound.

5. Read the text aloud once, following the signals as closely as possible. Critique yourself (and encourage students to comment) about how you might make your reading clearer and more expressive. Write notes for improvement on the transparency.

Signal	What It Tells the Reader to Do
Period (.)	Stop briefly
Exclamation mark (!)	Show surprise or excitement
Question mark (?)	Let voice go up
Comma (,)	Pause briefly
Quote marks (" ")	Shift speakers
Purpose of print	Tone of voice (funny, serious, etc.)
Ellipsis (...)	Pause
End of line	Sometimes pause

6. Finally, allow students to try out a number of different poems and/or songs to find the one they would like to present for their coffeehouse reading.

THREE-PART LESSON: POETRY CAFÉ

PART 2: IT TAKES PRACTICE

Explanation

In this three-part lesson, students develop fluency while experiencing favorite song lyrics or poetry verses in a new way. In this second part, students practice reading and rereading their selected piece as they prepare to present it during the culminating "coffeehouse." When students have a purpose for developing fluency, they'll more willingly use text signals to help them get their reading to sound right.

Skill Focus

Reading aloud with appropriate pacing, phrasing, intonation, rhythm, and rate; identifying rhymes, rhythm, and patterned structures in poetry

Materials & Resources

Text
- Popular or traditional songs and poems (Used in this three-part lesson: "The Erie Canal" from *Gonna Sing My Head Off!* collected by Kathleen Krull)

Other
- List of text signals from Part 1
- Transparency, with highlighting and notations from Part 1, of the selected song or poem

Bonus Ideas

Display pictures of poetry cafés of the past on a bulletin board to pique students' interest in what "coffeehouses" look like. Encourage students to explore the subject on the Internet (with your supervision) and to start to assemble a list of props.

STEPS

1. Using your list from Part 1, review the kinds of text signals that affect how readers adjust their voices as they read a piece of text. Discuss any new ideas students might have and add these to the list.

2. Next, display the transparency of the poem or song from Part 1. Review the highlighted items and the class's suggestions for improvement. Below is a small segment of the sample song, with some possible notes that might have been made in the previous lesson:

The Erie Canal

"I've got a mule, her name is Sal,"

I need to pause very briefly when I come to each comma.

"And we know ev'ry inch of the way from Albany to Buffalo."

There are some words in this song that are written incorrectly or as slang to let me know how they fit the rhythm of the song, like *ev'ry* instead of *every*. So I need to watch out for those.

I know I need to pause at the ends of these lines, especially where I see a period.

"Low bridge, ev'rybody down! Low bridge, for we're coming to a town!"

I'll need to make my voice sound excited here because I see exclamation marks!

---

3. Explain that real fluency develops only after much reading and rereading. Especially when a reader plans to read something aloud to others, he or she must put in a great deal of practice ahead of the performance. Therefore, you will keep yesterday's suggestions in mind as you read the song again. Present a final reading of your poem or song.

4. Now have students work independently with the poem or song they've selected. Ask them to underline or highlight any text signals they notice. Encourage them to read with appropriate emphasis and expression and to interpret the song or poem with feeling. Invite them to add notes to themselves to help them remember their interpretations.

5. After sufficient independent practice, allow time for students to read to a partner. This will give them experience in performing for others as well as provide them with additional feedback.

6. Set the date for the Poetry Café—this might be the next day, or it might be a few days hence: whenever your class has had adequate practice.

THREE-PART LESSON: POETRY CAFÉ

PART 3: PERFORMANCE DAY

Explanation

This culminating lesson gives students the opportunity they have been practicing for—the chance to be the spotlighted reader in a transformed classroom that feels and looks like a coffeehouse. Because students should be comfortable with their readings by now, they should have a lot of fun both as performers and as audience members. As we hope you'll discover, this lesson provides an example of reading for authentic purposes at its best!

Skill Focus

Reading aloud with appropriate pacing, phrasing, intonation, rhythm, and rate; identifying rhymes, rhythm, and patterned structures in poetry

Materials & Resources

Text

- Popular or traditional songs and poems (Used in this three-part lesson: "The Erie Canal" from *Gonna Sing My Head Off!* collected by Kathleen Krull)

Other

- Stool; spotlight for the reader (a gooseneck floor lamp works well)

- Sign ("Poetry Café") on the class door

- Drinks of coffee-flavored milk, cocoa, or juice for everyone

- Small cloths (festive dishcloths) or cloth napkins to cover desks/tables (although optional, these would enhance the experience)

- Berets (although optional, these would enhance the experience)

Prior to the Lesson: Getting your classroom ready for the Poetry Café celebration will take careful planning. You'll need to assemble your props ahead of time, and then, on the day itself, arrange the room appropriately. Cluster desks or tables to simulate the asymmetrical seating in a coffeehouse and, if you are using them, lay out your dishcloths or napkins to decorate the tables. Place the reader's stool at the front of the room and set up your lighting. You might want to form a committee of interested students who can help you with the different steps. It also works well if a few parents can help out—supplying, for instance, the beverages and/or beverage maker. These parents can play another important role, too—as audience members for your budding performers!

STEPS

1. By the time the Poetry Café day arrives, students should be well prepared to read their songs or poems with excellent fluency. Start the day by hanging the sign on your classroom door. This will alert everyone to the arrival of the special day.

2. With the room arranged and the props in place (see "Prior to the Lesson" notes above), turn off or lower the overhead lights and turn on the reader's "spotlight" next to the stool. With helpers, serve the drinks you've planned—cocoa, coffee-flavored milk, juice—to the participants. Welcome all to the Poetry Café.

3. You might want to be the first reader. This helps students ease into the process and feel more comfortable.

4. In either prearranged or random order, have each student come forward to read his or her selection. Lead in clapping after each performance.

5. Be sure to praise students' efforts, especially all the practice they have put in. Remind students that rereading text and paying attention to the signals are what develop fluency.

THREE-STEP SMART GUESSES

This lesson teaches students to quickly and consistently apply an effective three-step strategy for unfamiliar words. This is an activity that students can use in all content areas that involve reading, including math, science, health, and language arts.

Skill Focus

Using basic elements of phonetic analysis to read unfamiliar words; using structural cues to decode and understand text; using context clues to construct meaning; using syntax to construct meaning

Materials & Resources

Text

- A large-font book or a Big Book, either fiction or nonfiction (Used in this lesson: "The Cave of the One-Eyed Giant," a story from *The Odyssey* by Homer, illustrated by Bryan Pollard)

Other

- 3" x 3" sticky notes; scissors

Bonus Ideas

As a year-round reminder for students, construct a strategy chart to hang on your classroom wall. An example follows:

Three Steps for Making a Smart Guess About a New Word:

1. Ask yourself, "What makes sense here?"

2. Get your mouth ready for the first sound—everything before the first vowel.

3. Look at all of the letters and say them if you need to.

Prior to the Lesson: *Before the start of this lesson, read through the text you've chosen. Select about five or six words to mask out. Choose only words for which there is sufficient context (both syntactic and semantic) to allow students to make reasonable guesses about the word's identity. Place a sticky note, cut precisely to the size of the word, over each selected word. Next, make a snip with your scissors to create a flap in each sticky note. The flap should be cut so that, when lifted, it reveals only the beginning part of each word (all letters before the first vowel). See the diagram at right.*

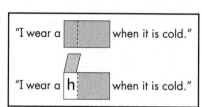

"I wear a _____ when it is cold."

"I wear a h____ when it is cold."

STEPS

1. Tell students that good readers—including adults—frequently encounter words in text that they don't know. When good readers come to these new words, they don't just make wild guesses about what the words might be. Instead, they make smart guesses! Today's lesson will show students how to use a three-step process to make these same smart guesses.

2. Read your selected book aloud, stopping when you come to words that are covered by the sticky notes. Model how you use the Three-Step Smart Guess strategy to figure out these words. A think-aloud for the sample book might sound like this:

Text	Teacher's Think-Aloud and Actions
Suddenly, a huge shadow, thrown by the setting sun, fell across the opening of the cave, and a [covered word] man entered.	*Encounter the word covered by the sticky note and stop to think aloud.* "Hmm...what makes sense here? It says this man's shadow was huge. Could the covered word also be *huge*? I think it's too long to be the word *huge*. Maybe it's *humongous*. Now let me look at the first part of the word and see if my guess is right." *Flip up the first part of the sticky note to reveal the letter* m. "No, the first part—everything before the first vowel—is *m*. That can't be *humongous*. Hmm...maybe he is like a monster. I need to change *monster* into an adjective. How about a *monstrous* man?" *Uncover the rest of the word.* "Hey! I was right—*monstrous* is the word. It helped to think through it!"

3. Use this procedure to model figuring out several words. Then challenge students to make smart guesses about several of the additional words you've covered with sticky notes. Praise their efforts!

4. Tell students that in the next lesson you'll give them a means of keeping this strategy, among several others, handy at all times.

BOOKMARKED: A VARIETY OF STRATEGIES TO DECODE AND UNDERSTAND

Explanation

Students need to realize that there are many different strategies they can use to decode unknown words. This lesson provides six possibilities (including the Three-Step Smart Guess strategy from the previous lesson), all summarized on a special, handy tool—a bookmark! You might consider sharing the bookmark with parents as well, along with directions about how they can use it to prompt their children during reading at home. This will help ensure exposure to the same strategies in different reading settings.

Skill Focus

Using basic elements of phonetic analysis to read unfamiliar words; using structural cues to decode and understand text; using context clues to construct meaning; using syntax to construct meaning

Materials & Resources

Text

- Transparencies of two brief text selections (fiction or nonfiction) that will allow you to model several different strategies for decoding unfamiliar words

Other

- 1 bookmark per student (photocopy the Decoding Strategies Bookmark Appendix, page 119, several times and cut the pages into strips to create bookmarks; if possible, laminate the bookmarks or back them with cardboard)

STEPS

1. Tell students that today they will have a chance to review six different strategies—including the three-step strategy they learned in the previous lesson—for figuring out unfamiliar words as they're reading. Because this is a lot to remember, you're going to give them a special tool that will help keep these strategies handy and available.

2. Distribute a bookmark to each student. Explain that each row is a separate strategy. When students encounter an unfamiliar word in text, they should consider the different strategies and then decide which one can best help them to read that word.

3. Display one text selection transparency. Read through it. Each time you encounter a difficult word, think aloud about how a reader might use the strategies on the bookmark to figure out that word. Below are excerpts from possible think-alouds for each bookmark strategy:

Strategy	Excerpt from Sample Teacher Think-Aloud
Put your finger on the word and say all the letters.	"Saying the letters helps me pay attention to the whole word."
Use the letters and the picture clues.	"I look at the pictures to see if any of those could match with words on that page."
Look for chunks of the word you know.	"Quite often there will be prefixes and suffixes, blends, endings, or other chunks of words that can help me figure out what the word is."
Keep your finger on the word and finish the sentence.	"By doing this, I check to see what would fit in this spot and make sense in the sentence."
Look for a rhyme you know.	"I know that words that sound alike can help me spell other words. They can also help me read other words. I look for the endings—the ending goes from the vowel to the last letter of the word."
Approach it as a Smart-Guess word.	"This reminds me to use the 'Three-Step Smart Guess' strategy." (see page 23)

4. Now display the second text selection transparency. Read it aloud, stopping at difficult words to apply an appropriate strategy. Each time you do this, have students place a finger on their bookmark to indicate the strategy that they think you've used to figure out the word.

OUTSTANDING HIGH-FREQUENCY WORDS

Explanation

Being able to instantly recognize high-frequency words greatly affects readers' (and writers') fluency and comprehension. Once students can automatically identify the words that occur most commonly in their reading and writing, they are no longer slowed by the process of deliberating over the encoding or decoding of these words. Regularly, you'll want to set aside time in your day to give students practice with these words.

Skill Focus

Recognizing and using common sight words appropriate to grade level

Materials & Resources

Text

- 1 page of fiction, appropriate for grade level and not densely filled with text

Other

- Transparency of the selected page of text

- Photocopies of the same page of text, 1 for each student

- Highlighters for students (optional)

Bonus Ideas

Use snowballs (even in hot weather!) to help students review high-frequency words. Call out a high-frequency word, have students write it quickly on a sheet of paper, and then make a snowball with the paper. Give them a signal to throw it in the air. (It's just paper and won't hurt anyone!) Everyone gets a snowball, opens it quickly, and checks it (with your help) for spelling. If the spelling is incorrect, they edit it.

STEPS

1. Tell students that teachers sometimes refer to "easy words" when they are thinking about text that their students read. Sometimes they might call these same words by a more sophisticated term—"high-frequency words." Both phrases describe these words accurately: Because they are used all the time in text, they occur with high frequency. And because they're so common and familiar, they're easy to recognize. In fact, that's the goal for easy words: Readers need to be able to recognize them instantly. Words like *a*, *and*, and *the* are some of the most frequently encountered high-frequency words.

2. Now write the following sentence on the board or on a transparency:

   How many easy words are included in what we read?

3. Point to each word in the sentence and discuss with the class whether it should be considered a high-frequency word. Highlight those that you deem high frequency. (Although there's room for some debate, it's likely you would highlight: *how*, *many*, *are*, *in*, *what*, and *we*.)

4. Call attention to the fact that most of the words in this sentence—six out of ten—are high-frequency words. Point out that a reader who knew the high-frequency words in this sentence would be able to read it quickly and efficiently. This is true of a great deal of our reading (and writing).

5. Give each student a copy of the text you've chosen. Say something like, "We've tried this experiment with a sentence. Now, let's see if our experiment works with longer pieces of text." Have students form pairs or small groups. Ask them to talk together and decide which words are used often in the books and stories they read. Caution them that some discussion about the words is fine, but that no words are worth arguing about. Once they've made their decisions, they are to highlight or underline the words on the page.

6. Now have partners or groups switch papers to compare their own decisions with other students' choices. Rotate the papers so that each group has a chance to compare their decisions with those made by all other groups.

7. Bring the class back together. Have a volunteer from each group present their words to the class. There should be a good deal of overlap among the groups' findings—in fact, in fiction at this grade level, high-frequency words typically account for about half of all of the text. Conclude by stressing how important the "easy" words are for our rate and understanding as readers.

PRACTICING WITH HIGH-FREQUENCY WORDS—SWAT IT

Explanation

This lesson provides a great follow-up to the previous lesson on high-frequency words. In fact, this one may have your students practically begging to practice their high-frequency words! It may appear to be simply a game to students, but it really provides excellent experience in quick word recognition.

Skill Focus

Recognizing and using common sight words appropriate to grade level

Materials & Resources

Text

- List you've compiled of 25 commonly used words that your students often stumble over in their daily reading and/or continually misspell in their rough draft writing

Other

- 2 sheets of poster paper

- About 50 precut, designer sticky notes or die-cut figures (stars, apples, etc.)

- 2 flyswatters (Note: Most dollar stores stock novelty swatters that are fun for students—for instance, flip-flop swatters or hand-shaped swatters)

Bonus Ideas

The Swat It! activity has many variations. For example, write all the possible answers to the multiplication table the class is currently memorizing. Call out a problem and have students swat the answer. Or, create a chart of vocabulary words for content areas or literature and call out definitions.

Prior to the Lesson: Before the start of the lesson, you'll need to make the "Swat It" posters. Place the designer sticky notes or die-cut shapes randomly on each sheet of poster paper. Laminate and trim both sheets. Using a wide-tip marker, print one of the targeted 25 words on each shape. Be sure to write the same words on both charts in different positions. (See photograph on page 18.)

STEPS

1. Review with students the importance of their knowing high-frequency words automatically. Sum up the basic reason this way: Students will become better readers and writers if they can instantly recognize and use these words because they account for a great proportion of the overall words needed for reading and writing.

2. Mount the two charts a foot or so apart on the chalkboard or a bulletin board. Explain that the class is going to play a game so that you can check to see whether they know the words on the chart.

3. Then form two teams and line up the teams so that each is facing a chart. Give a flyswatter to the first person on each team.

4. Tell students that this is how the game works: You'll call out a word that will be in a different position on each chart. The first person in each line is to search for and swat that word. As soon as he or she swats the word, the flyswatter passes to the next student in line and the original student moves to the end of the line to await another turn. You'll award and record a point for the team that swats the correct word first. The game is over when each team member has had at least a couple of turns.

5. After you've played the game and celebrated the winning team (and the other team's efforts), remind students how important high-frequency words are. Knowing these simple words will help them to be quicker and better at reading and writing!

DIFFERENT MEANINGS IN DIFFERENT CONTEXTS

Explanation

Exploring words with multiple meanings is a lot of fun. This lesson provides just a few of the many guessing game possibilities for teaching these words. As students sort through definitions to determine which to apply in different situations, they are expanding and enriching their word knowledge. The many Amelia Bedelia stories are a great way to introduce these words to your students. No doubt your students will be surprised by how many words in our language have multiple meanings. And their vocabularies will grow accordingly!

Skill Focus

Applying different meanings in different contexts

Materials & Resources

Text

- Any Amelia Bedelia series book (Used in this lesson: *Amelia Bedelia's Family Album* by Peggy Parrish)

Other

- Sheet of unlined paper, 1 for each student; crayons; markers

Bonus Ideas

Cut apart copies of several students' sheets so that you have individual cells (for each word, there should be at least two separate cells, each representing a different meaning). Distribute a cell to each student. Have students form a circle. Allow each student to pretend to "be" his or her word. Challenge students to figure out, based on the charades, which other student(s) have the same word that they have.

STEPS

1. Explain to students that many words in the English language have several different meanings. Being familiar with the different meanings helps readers more readily figure out which meaning applies in a particular sentence. For example, the word *wave* can mean "an ocean swell" or "a hand signal," and the word *light* can mean "not heavy" or "a lamp."

2. Tell students that you'll provide further illustrations by drawing pairs of pictures. Each picture pair can be described by the same word. Their job is to guess that word. Below is a sample list you might provide (answers are provided for your convenience):

[Your sketch of several fish]	[Your sketch of a schoolhouse]
(*school*)	(*school*)
[Your sketch of a bird's beak]	[Your sketch of a restaurant check]
(*bill*)	(*bill*)
[Your sketch of a leg or an arm]	[Your sketch of a tree branch]
(*limb*)	(*limb*)
[Your sketch of a baseball hat]	[Your sketch of a bottle cap]
(*cap*)	(*cap*)

3. Now tell students that today's story contains many words like this. Life gets very confusing when the character misinterprets these multiple meanings!

4. Distribute a sheet of paper to each student. Have them fold it in half four times and then unfold it. This should create a grid with sixteen cell divisions.

5. Read the selected story through once just for students' enjoyment. Then read it again, pausing after each paragraph to allow students time to record the words with multiple meanings. Have them write the words twice—once in each of two cells. Stop reading when students have completed their charts—that is, after you have encountered eight multiple-meaning words.

6. Make available crayons and markers. Invite students to depict the two different meanings of each word by either drawing illustrations or by writing definitions (or perhaps by doing both) in the appropriate grid cells. (Note that many multiple-meaning words have more than two meanings; accept whichever two appropriate meanings students determine.)

Monitoring Comprehension

Too often students pick up a book and engage in what seems like reading. However, what is actually happening is that they are "calling" words. They may be calling words with accuracy and clarity and they may do so from the start to the finish of a whole book, but if they are not understanding what the words mean, they are not really reading. Genuine reading is a complex process that involves a multitude of cognitive activities. Put most succinctly, reading is thinking.

In *I Read It, but I Don't Get It*, Cris Tovani (2000) calls attention to the fact that we have two voices that work in tandem during reading—one voice saying the words and one responding to the words. Readers have to activate both voices to be successfully, genuinely reading. Some students don't do this automatically. They need direct instruction to become aware of the intricacies of reading.

The lessons in this section teach second and third graders to be metacognitive, or self-aware, in their reading. The research of Harris and Hodges (1995) defines this as "knowing when what one is reading makes sense by monitoring and controlling one's own comprehension" (p. 39). Only when students become keenly aware of their own thinking during reading will they be able to recognize problems. Awareness is the key first step; having effective strategies at hand is the second. Thus, the underlying goals of all the lessons in this section can be summed up as follows:

- to enable students to assess their own understanding and evaluate their assumptions as they read; and

- to encourage increasing independence in students' practice and application of self-monitoring and self-correct strategies.

Sitting with students and guiding them as they apply strategies to text is an early step along the way to students' self-monitoring their reading.

With these goals in mind, the section offers lessons with a variety of emphases on evaluating text and monitoring comprehension. Students experience a range of critical thinking activities—from techniques for pausing during reading to assess ongoing understanding to differentiating statements of fact and opinion to keeping track of characters and relationships in a story. In one lesson, they get "behind the wheel" and discover how important it is to catch themselves if they've become distracted during reading and have "run off the road." In another lesson, they are introduced to "KNOW" and "GO" words and to a process that can help them determine the importance of a specific word relative to understanding the overall text. In yet another, they learn a rereading and retelling "fix-it" strategy.

Second and third graders are ready for these kinds of activities. With your guidance, they will grow into readers who can navigate text successfully. And those are readers who love to read and love to learn.

This teacher coaches a small group of students as they use tools from their tool kits to help them process text.

HEARING THE TWO VOICES OF A GOOD READER

Explanation

Many beginning readers have not yet learned the true purpose of reading—that the reader must go beyond merely saying words to making sense of the text and constructing meaning. A critical part of constructing meaning is thinking actively during the process of reading the words. In a dynamic activity, this lesson introduces and reinforces that concept.

Skill Focus

Self-monitoring comprehension; using appropriate self-correct strategies; understanding and identifying what good readers do

Materials & Resources

Text

- Brief fiction or nonfiction text of at least 5–6 sentences (Used in this lesson: excerpt from *Twisters and Other Terrible Storms* by Will Osborne and Mary Pope Osborne, p. 44)

Other

- Transparency of the text

- Tape recorder with a Pause button; a recording of the text in your own voice

Bonus Ideas

To give students practice with their two voices, put partners together—designating one the reader and one the recorder. The "human recorder" holds out both fists—one for the Pause button and the other for the Start button. The reader reads aloud until his/her other voice is ready to respond at which time he/she presses the "Pause button" and speaks. Then, when ready to read again, the reader presses the "Start button" and continues.

Prior to the Lesson: Make a recording of the text you've selected for the lesson. Be sure to read slowly but fluently as you record.

STEPS

1. Ask students to guess how many voices they should hear as they read to themselves. After several students have shared their thoughts, explain that good readers have two very distinct voices, even when they are reading silently! Today you're going to demonstrate both of the voices you hear in your head each time you read.

2. Display the transparency. Tell students that one of your reading voices simply says the words of the text. Every time you read, you hear this voice in your head clearly. Say something like, "Here's what this voice sounds like to me as I read." Press the tape recorder button and play the recording all the way through.

3. Ask students, "How many of you hear yourselves reading that way in your own head?" Hopefully, many, if not all, will reply that they hear their voices reading in this way.

4. Now tell students that you'll demonstrate the other voice that you hear in addition to that first voice. You call this your "reading-thinking voice." Play the recording again, this time hitting the Pause button periodically to think aloud about what you've just read. Below is the sample text, with an example of a self-monitoring script:

Sample Text, as Recorded ("Reading Voice")	Model of Teacher's Script, Based on Sample ("Reading-Thinking Voice")
Lightning can jump from place to place inside a cloud. It can shoot from one cloud to another. (**Pause 1**) It can also jump from a cloud to the ground. That's when it's really dangerous! (**Pause 2**) Lightning is hot! Meteorologists think a bolt of lightning can be five times as hot as the surface of the sun. (**Pause 3**) When lightning flashes, the great heat causes the air around the flash to expand very quickly. The expanding air makes a sound like an explosion. (**Pause 4**)	**Pause 1:** I've seen that happen when I've been on a plane that's in a thunderstorm! It's really beautiful, but it's a little scary, too! **Pause 2:** I guess when it jumps to the ground that's when people and homes are sometimes struck. I know lightning can kill people and burn down homes. **Pause 3:** Wow! I can't imagine how hot that is! **Pause 4:** I know that's what we call thunder. I didn't realize that was what made the noise, though!

5. Review with students that a good reader's second voice expresses thoughts about the words and begins to make sense of those words.

CODING TEXT: SHOWING THE TRACKS OF A READER

Explanation

This lesson reinforces the critical message taught in the previous lesson: true reading means making meaning, not just calling words. And a fundamental part of making meaning is monitoring one's thoughts during reading. This lesson emphasizes that concept quite graphically!

Skill Focus

Self-monitoring comprehension; using appropriate self-correct strategies; asking and answering questions about texts; understanding and identifying what good readers do

Materials & Resources

Text

- Any grade-appropriate brief fiction or nonfiction text of at least 5–6 sentences (Used in this lesson: "Aall Aabout Aardvarks" by Jeananda Col)

Other

- Transparency of the selected text
- A blank transparency
- Photocopies, 1 for each student, of text similar to that on the text transparency

Bonus Ideas

In order to use this activity with text materials that students can't write on, provide sticky notes that you've snipped into strips. Students can use these sticky notes to write their symbols, and they can place the strips in the appropriate spots in the text.

STEPS

1. Display the blank transparency. Tell students that you're going to draw something and you want them to guess what it is. Draw a set of animal paw prints, as shown at right:

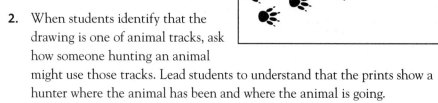

2. When students identify that the drawing is one of animal tracks, ask how someone hunting an animal might use those tracks. Lead students to understand that the prints show a hunter where the animal has been and where the animal is going.

3. Tell students that today's lesson will involve the tracks that they, as readers, leave on a printed page. Display the transparency. Superimpose on it the transparency of the animal tracks and say, "Today I'll be able to see exactly where you've been as a reader—just the way a hunter tracks an animal!"

4. Review the types of things good readers think about. Start with the four basic categories listed below. On the board or poster paper, write the following phrases and symbols and discuss each. (Note: If you feel that four symbols will overwhelm your students, you might try just one or two a day.)

    - Things I already knew ✔
    - Things that are new to me *
    - Things that surprise me !
    - Things that I have questions about ?

5. Write the same symbols on the top of the text transparency. Read the text aloud slowly, stopping occasionally to place an appropriate symbol next to the text to represent your thinking. An example follows:

    > "I never knew that aardvarks had a super-sticky saliva that they use to get ants from under the ground! That's pretty cool!" (Place a "!" alongside that fact.)

6. Proceed in this way through several paragraphs of the text. At the conclusion of your modeling, mention again the "tracks" analogy, pointing out how by now the text shows the "tracks" of where you've been as a reader—how you were thinking and processing text.

7. Distribute the text photocopies to students. Have them read and insert appropriate symbols to show their thinking. Be sure that students know that they aren't always expected to use all the symbols.

It's a Matter of Opinion . . . or Fact!

Explanation

All too often, young readers equate print and truth–if it's in print, it must be true! This lesson exposes the fallacy of that thinking. To become discriminating readers, students need to be aware that one of their most important jobs is analyzing and evaluating text and making ongoing decisions about what they're reading.

Skill Focus

Distinguishing between fact and opinion; self-monitoring comprehension and using self-correct strategies; identifying what good readers do

Materials & Resources

Text

- A fiction or nonfiction text selection that contains facts and opinions

Other

- 2 sets of sentence strips containing facts and opinions
- Pocket chart
- 2 word cards with chart headings

Bonus Ideas

To show students that their opinions are important, create a bulletin board entitled, "Our Opinions Matter." Encourage all students to write a sentence that includes one of their opinions. Provide several stems, such as, "The best school lunch is ____"; "The best story we've read so far this year is ____"; or "The most talented movie star is ____." Have students write their sentences on strips that can be posted for all to see.

Prior to the Lesson: Create one set of sentence strips with statements of fact and opinion relating to your students and a second set with fact and opinion statements relating to the selected text. Create, as well, a pocket chart and two headings, on word cards, for the chart. One card should say "Fact" and the other "Opinion."

STEPS

1. Gather students around you. Explain that in today's lesson the class will explore facts and opinions and will figure out the difference between these two kinds of statements. Display the pocket chart. With students watching, place the "Fact" and "Opinion" word cards in the appropriate heading slots.

2. Lay the student-related sentence strips face down on a desk. Tell students that this pile contains an assortment of both fact and opinion statements. You will ask volunteers to pick a strip, read it to the class, and decide whether it is fact or opinion. Say something like, "To help you make your decision, for each strip I want you to ask yourself: 'Is this something that everyone—even people who aren't in our class—could agree is true?' "

3. Call on different volunteers, guiding students as needed to place each strip in the appropriate chart column. Below is a sample list of assorted statements (answers are provided for your convenience):

   Andy wears glasses. (fact)

   Mrs. Lovett's dress is cool! (opinion)

   Lucy has a turtle. (fact)

   The best pet is a turtle. (opinion)

4. With students' input, make a list of clues that can help a reader decide whether a text statement is fact or opinion. Write the list on the board or a poster chart. Guide students to include criteria like the following:

   - A fact is something that everyone knows is true.

   - A fact is something we can prove is true.

   - An opinion is what one or more people think, feel, or believe.

   - An opinion often includes words like "I think..." or "We believe..." to show that personal views are being expressed.

5. Now tell students that they'll have a chance to find facts and opinions in a reading selection. Set up partner groups and distribute to each a text-related sentence strip. Partners are to read the selected text together and to figure out which parts of the text are fact and which are opinion. They should also check to see what the text reveals about their sentence strip: Is it a statement of fact or opinion?

6. Finally, have students re-gather at the pocket chart. Invite each pair to place their strip in the appropriate column and to explain their decision.

HERE'S WHAT I THINK

Scholastic Teaching Resources

Explanation

Stopping during reading and thinking about what one has just read is a critical metacognitive skill. It enables the reader to evaluate what he or she has really understood. Getting young students to do this, however, is a challenge. Their tendency is to read right through a piece. This lesson models how and why they must learn to stop and take stock.

Skill Focus

Self-monitoring comprehension and using self-correct strategies; understanding and identifying what good readers do; recalling details in text

Materials & Resources

Text

- A brief, easy-to-read fiction or nonfiction text selection

Other

- 1 sticky note, snipped into 5 "fingers," for each student and for the teacher

Bonus Ideas

The ultimate goal is to have students use "I Think" independently during their free choice and assigned reading—without the sticky notes and without talking aloud. This will likely take lots of practice! As a step along the way, encourage them to use their whisper voices to think aloud when they reach their sticky notes and to gradually reduce the number of notes.

STEPS

1. Explain to students that good readers stop occasionally to think more about what they've read. They take time to be sure they've understood the words they've just read. Explain further that many readers often forget to do this. They wind up getting confused or lost. To help students remember, you're going to teach them a useful strategy called "I Think."

2. Display the selected text and model for students how you place the sticky note strips at random spots throughout the section you're planning to read. Tell students that the sticky notes will serve as your reminders to stop. (Point out that, although your placement is random in the sense that it is not based on content, you're positioning the notes at logical places—for example, every other paragraph or once per column of text.)

3. Read aloud until you get to the first sticky note. Stop and say, "I think…" Retell what you've just read, reflect on what you've read, make predictions, and/or ask questions. Conclude your think-aloud with, "I understand really well what I'm reading about so far. I know that I'm thinking as I read and that's important."

4. Continue to read and think aloud. Read enough material to give the students a real feel for how the process works and for doing their own think-alouds.

5. Tell students it's their turn. Identify the section of text you want them to read (a different section from the one you used to model so that students don't rely too heavily on your thoughts). Organize students into partner groups and distribute a set of sticky note strips to each group. Have them follow your model, placing the strips randomly throughout the text. Suggest that partners take turns—one partner at a time gets to stop and explain what they think they've read.

FIXING YOUR READING

Explanation

Like the previous lesson, this lesson teaches students the importance of pausing and retelling to check comprehension during reading. However, here the focus is on situations in which comprehension has broken down. Students learn a helpful strategy for fixing problems as they occur.

Skill Focus

Self-monitoring comprehension and using self-correct strategies; understanding and identifying what good readers do; recalling details in text; rereading to clarify

Materials & Resources

Text

- A brief fiction or nonfiction text selection, somewhat more challenging than the selection used in the previous lesson

Other

- 1 sticky note, snipped into 5 "fingers," for each student and for the teacher

Bonus Ideas

Create a poster for the classroom with the fix-up strategies listed. Students can use it to support their reading. Refer to it often in your own modeling.

- I'll reread and rethink.
- I'll ask more questions as I read this time.
- I'll see if I can picture what I'm reading.
- I'll pay attention to conventions that may help me.
- I'll use the text to make connections.

STEPS

1. Review the previous day's lesson in which students learned that good readers stop occasionally in their reading to retell and reflect on what they've read. Explain that today's lesson will pick up from that lesson: Using a similar procedure, students will learn what to do if they discover they cannot retell what they've just read or if the retelling doesn't make sense. Today's fix-it strategy will teach them a way to get back on track.

2. Tell students that in this strategy, you will not place sticky notes ahead of time to remind you to pause. Instead, you will just stop at a reasonable interval of text—for instance, at the beginning or ending of a page or column or paragraph. (Note: Reasonable intervals vary according to the denseness and complexity of a particular piece of text.)

3. Display the selected text and read aloud until you reach a reasonable interval. Stop and retell, successfully, what you have just read. Say something like, "I feel like I understand what I just read. So I'm going to put a sticky note here to remind me that up until this point I have understood this text." Place a sticky note at that point.

4. Continue your reading until you reach another reasonable interval. This time attempt a retelling, but make it a bit disjointed and skeletal. It should reveal unanswered questions that show your confusion.

5. Now tell students that because you haven't understood this part of the text, you will return to the place you marked with a sticky note. Explain that this makes sense because you know that up until that sticky note, you had understood the text. So, somewhere in between that spot and the second interval, your comprehension broke down.

6. Go back to the sticky note and reread the text that you didn't fully comprehend. Say something like, "It's great to have a marker to guide me back to a specific spot or else I might need to start all the way over again!" Reread the text that you haven't understood and demonstrate for students how by rereading and rethinking the material, you are able to understand it better. Provide a new, more coherent retelling to demonstrate your improved comprehension. Explain that sometimes readers do not sufficiently improve their comprehension by rereading. If so, there are a number of additional fix-it strategies they might try. (See Bonus Ideas for suggested chart of the strategies. You can create new mini-lessons, based on the model provided in this lesson, to demonstrate each of these strategies.)

7. Distribute a set of sticky note fingers to each student. During today's independent or assigned reading, have students practice what you've modeled.

RUNNING OFF THE ROAD!

Explanation

This lesson uses an extended metaphor to heighten students' awareness of the ways in which readers can go off course during reading. Through self-monitoring, readers learn to refocus on their reading and to ignore distractions that can interfere with comprehension.

Skill Focus

Self-monitoring comprehension and using self-correct strategies; understanding and identifying what good readers do; rereading to clarify

Materials & Resources

Text

- Any grade-appropriate brief fiction or nonfiction text of at least 5–6 sentences

Other

- Transparency of the selected text

- Transparency marker

- 1 sticky note, snipped into 5 "fingers," for each student

Bonus Ideas

Using simple clip art of cars, make a bookmark for each of your students. Title the bookmark "Stay on the Reading Road!" Give these to students as reminders that they shouldn't let their minds wander as they read. Students should keep these bookmarks in their toolkits and use them to mark different items such as clues, stopping places, or favorite pages.

STEPS

1. Ask students if they've ever played a video game that simulates driving a car. Surely some will respond that they've done so. Now ask if they've ever had the experience of running off the road with that car. Expand the discussion to include the observation that sometimes real drivers run off the road, too. Sometimes this can cause serious accidents, although usually drivers quickly correct their mistake and steer back onto the road.

2. Continue by encouraging students to explain why people might occasionally steer off a road. Guide the discussion to include the fact that drivers' minds might be focused on things other than their driving—maybe what to fix for supper, how to solve a problem, or a job they need to do. Expand the conversation to include readers: Tell students that readers can also "run off the road." Readers do this for the same reason that drivers do it—they have their minds on something other than the text. The penalty for a reader who runs off the road isn't as risky as for a motorist, but it still can cause problems.

3. Display the transparency. On the left side of the page just above the top margin, draw an outline of a car. Then, in the left margin, draw a wavy line (to indicate a road) from the car to the bottom of the page. Tell students that you're going to model for them what happens to a reader whose mind isn't on what he or she is reading. Read the text aloud, occasionally stopping to make comments such as, "You know, I haven't gotten the lunch count to the office yet today. I'd better do that as soon as we finish our lesson," or "I've got to remember to go by the grocery store on the way home this afternoon. I need a loaf of bread." Each time you model a digression, use the transparency pen to mark an X on the wavy line. Each X indicates a spot where you veered from your reading road.

4. Be sure students realize that "running off the road" during reading happens to everyone at some point. Good readers monitor themselves by paying careful attention to their silent voices (the reading-thinking voice examined in the lesson on page 30) and watching out for signs that their minds have wandered. When that happens, they make sure they "get back on the road" and they check to make sure they haven't lost comprehension.

5. Challenge students to self-monitor their independent or assigned reading today. Distribute sticky note strips to each student. As they read, have them place a sticky note at all spots where they catch themselves thinking about something other than the text. Warn them that too many sticky notes probably means they aren't truly understanding what they are reading. If they only run off the road a time or two, they can probably get where they're going as readers!

KNOW OR GO WORDS

STEPS

1. Write these words on the board:

diffidence	cadaverous	quixotic
phlegmatic	raconteur	conveyance
perfidious	sanguinary	recriminate

2. Students will undoubtedly admit that they don't know these words and that even pronouncing them correctly would be very difficult. Tell students that many adults (yourself included, if that's the case!) wouldn't recognize all these words if they encountered them in a text.

3. Now ask the class to guess what story these difficult words came from. After some guesses, make another surprising revelation: They're all from the classic tale *Peter Pan*—a children's story! You might add, "This book has been enjoyed by boys and girls, as well as men and women, for many years. We've loved its great story and its beautiful language. But, not all of us have understood all of its words."

4. Explain that good readers often encounter words they don't know. In these instances, good readers figure out if the word is an important word. They determine if the word is a "KNOW" word or a "GO" word. Write "KNOW" and "GO" on the board. Next to each word, write its description, as follows:

   - **KNOW –** These words are very important. You'll find that you've lost comprehension just after you see them. You've got to go back and figure them out!

   - **GO –** These are good words but they aren't truly important for understanding what you've read. You'll find that you haven't lost comprehension after you meet them. Just keep going!

5. Tell students that to help them learn how to tell the difference between the two kinds of words, you'll demonstrate the process. Read an excerpt of text and model how you monitor your comprehension after encountering difficult words. An example dialogue, based on the sample text, is on the next page (targeted words are underlined).

Although the point of this lesson is to teach students that NO words can be "abandoned" during the reading of a particular selection, we don't want to convey the message that these words are unimportant. In fact, we want students to be curious about *all* words and to pursue their meanings and derivations when it's appropriate. To do this, you might want to make a "Wondrous Words" box for your classroom. Invite students to jot down any words they find interesting, especially during their independent self-selected reading time, and place these words in the box. Gather the whole class for a few minutes several times a week. Invite students to choose a word from the box to discuss. Keep a dictionary handy and ask that students help you find out more about the word and its uses. You might even want to use a colorful window marker (the kind that can be easily wiped off) to write these new words on your classroom windows. They will be visible to all for a few days and, best of all, they will enrich students' vocabulary every time they look out the window!

Sample Text	Teacher's Think-Aloud
He passed an aircraft carrier, <u>*Intrepid*</u>.	"That's a big word—*Intrepid*. I think, from the way it's written and positioned in this sentence, that it's the name of the aircraft carrier. Usually being able to pronounce a name isn't important. I think that this is a GO word."
Two ferries were leaving their <u>slips</u>.	"I know one meaning for the word *slip*—an article of clothing. But that doesn't make sense here. It must have another meaning. I think the key thing here is that the ferries 'were leaving,' but I'll pay extra-close attention as I keep reading and I'll come back to this if I have to. For now, it's a GO word."
The ferries . . . <u>veered</u> off their courses and avoided a <u>collision</u> with Henry!	"There are two difficult words in this sentence and I can't really make sense of the sentence without them. I'll read ahead just a bit. [Read the next couple of sentences and reveal that you are still confused.] Hmm. . . I think I'd better go back to that sentence with the two words and figure them out. They turn out to be KNOW words."

6. Distribute photocopies of a few pages of the sample text to students. Challenge them to read the text carefully and to monitor their comprehension closely when they encounter unknown words. Have them jot down KNOW words on one sticky note and GO words on the other sticky note.

7. Conclude by inviting students to place their sticky notes next to the appropriate KNOW or GO descriptions (see Step 4). Have students discuss why they designated particular words as they did.

MINI-LESSON

TWO-PART LESSON: WHO'S WHO

PART 1: IDENTIFYING CHARACTERS

Explanation

Not infrequently, readers are surprised to encounter a character who seems new to a story they are reading. Actually, the character was introduced earlier and should be familiar by now. Naturally, confusion results and comprehension suffers. In this series of two lessons, students will first identify a story's characters and distinguish them as main or minor. Then they'll progress to learning how to keep track of all the characters they've encountered.

Skill Focus

Self-monitoring comprehension and using self-correct strategies; understanding and identifying what good readers do; recalling details in text; identifying characters in a literary work

Materials & Resources

Text

- A narrative text that includes a main character and several minor characters, for instruction, and additional similar text(s) for students' work (Used in this lesson: "Cinderella")

Other

- Chalkboard, poster paper, or transparencies for your character wheel

- Sheet of unlined paper, 1 for each student for students' webs

(*Note: Be sure to preserve both the "Cinderella" character wheel and students' character webs; they will be needed in Part 2 of this lesson.*)

STEPS

1. Draw a stick-person figure on the board or on a transparency. Above it write the words "Main Character." Explain that the main character is the most important one in the story—the one around which the story revolves.

2. Share the following tips for identifying the main character of a story. You might write them on the board or poster paper for students to refer to later.

    The main character is . . .

    - in the story more than others

    - part of the problem of the story

    - part of the solution of the story

    - the person the story is mainly about

3. Tell students that you'll be using a familiar fairy tale, "Cinderella," as the basis of this lesson. Using the criteria you've listed on the board (and not simply the title), identify the main character as Cinderella. Write the name "Cinderella" under the stick figure you've drawn.

4. Now draw several stick-person figures encircling the main character. Write "Minor Characters" to the side of the drawing. Tell students that stories usually have one or more additional characters besides the main one. These minor characters have several roles—for instance, they help move the story's action (plot) along and they also help readers understand the main character better.

5. Call on students to identify the minor characters in "Cinderella." You might discuss briefly what readers learn about the main character from each of these lesser characters. Label each character as students identify him or her. A sample diagram is at right.

6. Distribute a sheet of unlined paper to each student. Have them read a self-selected or assigned narrative text and identify the main character and the minor characters. Following your model, they are to sketch one large stick figure and as many smaller ones as needed and then to label each appropriately.

Main Character · Fairy Godmother · Prince · Stepmother · Cinderella · Mouse · Stepsister · Stepsister · Minor Character

PART 2: MONITORING CHARACTERS AND THEIR RELATIONSHIPS

STEPS

1. Review your stick-person character wheel from the previous lesson. Call attention to how many characters a reader has to hold in his mind while reading (in "Cinderella" there are at least six). Discuss why it is important for a reader to be able to recall each character and understand why he or she is in the story.

2. Explain that as text increases in complexity and length, readers often need to pay attention to dozens of characters. Thus, many adult readers have had this experience: A character in a book is introduced at about the same point as other characters. Before they realize it, they are confused about who's who! They find themselves leafing back through earlier pages to figure things out. This is time-consuming and disruptive. Today you're going to show students a way to keep track of who the characters are so their comprehension won't be disrupted this way.

3. Display the Cinderella character wheel from yesterday's lesson. Begin to read aloud or retell the story. As you come to each character, draw a line to connect him or her to Cinderella. Briefly describe how that character interacts with the main character and helps the story to develop. At right is a sample diagram.

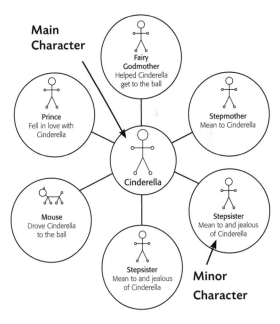

4. Now ask students to get out their own character wheels from Part 1 of this lesson. Have them reread the story and follow your model to add spokes and descriptions to the wheels.

5. Bring the class back together and invite them to compare and discuss their character wheels. As you close the lesson, remind students that making character wheels like this can be even more helpful in the future, as the texts they read will become increasingly complex.

Generating and Answering Questions

The best readers are questioners. Indeed, Albert Einstein could have been describing good readers when he said of himself, "I have no special talent. I am only passionately curious." From the moment good readers hold a book in their hands, they start to formulate questions. They ask themselves:

- What kind of book do I think this is?

- Have I read other books by this author?

- What were they about?

- Do I know anything about this topic?

And that's just the beginning—the pre-reading part. During reading, good readers are continually generating questions about the meaning of the text. In a fictional piece, they are wondering what a character will do next or how one plot twist will connect to another. In a nonfiction piece, they are assimilating facts that lead to unanticipated discoveries and further questions about those discoveries. It's an unending process, during which some questions are answered as others are formulated. And, often after the reading is done, unanswered questions remain. This simply means good readers have further inquiry, reading, and research ahead. In fact, a recurring series of questions and answers is what good reading is all about.

It follows, therefore, that instruction that focuses on questioning will improve students' reading. As the National Reading Panel reports: There is "strong empirical and scientific evidence that instruction of question generation during reading benefits reading comprehension in terms of memory and answering questions based on text as well as integrating and identifying main ideas through summarization" (2000, p. 4-88).

This student is using sticky notes placed by the teacher. The notes indicate where students are to stop reading and generate a question.

This section covers questioning from many different angles. Although narrative text still plays a central role, informational text becomes quite important in grades 2–3. Therefore, many of these lessons highlight content area and other kinds of expository reading. At these grade levels, students increasingly benefit from independent work. Thus, the lessons frequently call on them to generate their own questions and search for answers. Second and third graders are also growing in their ability to engage in abstract thinking, which can deepen the kinds of questions they can handle. The lessons allow them to experience how powerful questioning can be in clarifying their thinking.

The TV screen in this classroom displays Point and Ponder questions that guide students as they read an assigned text.

One set of lessons invites students to play an extended "I Bet . . ." game-like activity (with a metacognitive twist) as they preview a book. In addition to posing pre-reading questions and making predictions about a book, they also examine their own questions to understand how they might become better questioners.

In another series of lessons, students learn to judge whether a book is "just right" for them by asking five different questions. Each question helps them focus on a different aspect of the book—from word knowledge to fluency to level of thinking required—so that in the end they can successfully determine how well suited a particular book is for their own reading level. And in the process they are learning how to formulate excellent questions!

Young students are naturally curious. From the time they enter a classroom in the morning, they burst forth with a constant barrage of Who? What? Why? When? Where? and How? A good teacher can take that enthusiasm and curiosity and turn it to the child's great benefit in reading. It doesn't always make for a quiet, predictable classroom, but after all, we don't want them to be quiet, passive learners: encouraging the "noise" and the questions is part of the good teacher's job. We wish for all students that their natural passionate curiosity be sparked and developed as they learn how to ask and answer the best kinds of questions. The lessons in this section should help them do just that. Have fun!

WORD STACKS

Fold, then cut

shelter	chimney
mitten	blanket
ocean	snow
diagonal	fat
skiing	spray
orange	storage
lions	seals

Prior to the Lesson: *Locate key words in the selected text. Generate, as well, a list of about a dozen words that are not in the text—some of these words should demonstrate a close, or at least a potential, connection to the text topic while others should show no connection at all. Print or type the words in two-columns on a sheet of paper. Photocopy one sheet for each student or student group. Fold the sheet vertically down the middle and snip the paper from the outer edges to within about ¾" of the center fold. (See diagram.) Then unfold the sheet and cut up the center fold line to within 1" of the top. (You can fold and cut several sheets at a time.) The pages will remain intact until the word strips are pulled apart.*

STEPS

1. Read aloud the title of the sample text. Tell students that when good readers see or hear the title of a piece they're considering reading, they immediately begin to ask themselves what they expect to find in the text.

2. Hold up the sheet of words and demonstrate how easily you can pull apart each of the words (because you have precut them on the dotted lines). Place the words randomly in front of you.

3. Explain that you're going to look at each word to decide whether—based on the title—you think the word will be in the selection. You'll make one stack of words that you expect to find in the text, and another stack of words that you think won't appear in the text. For example, you might choose the word *shelter* and comment, "I know something about igloos— they are shelters against the cold for Eskimos. So, I expect to find this word in the text." Start one stack with the word, choose another word, and model your thinking. For example, you might say, "Hmm, *orange* . . . I don't know how the word *orange* could be used in a piece about building igloos. So, I'm going to put it in the stack of words that I *don't* expect to find. I'm calling that a 'trick word!' " Model two more words this way.

4. Arrange students either with partners or in small groups. Distribute a word sheet to each group. Instruct them to pull apart the individual words, just as you demonstrated.

5. Challenge students to sort their word cards into two stacks: words they might find in the text and "trick words" that don't seem connected to the text at all. Tell them that they should be able to discuss and justify why they have sorted words as they have.

6. Now have students read the text. Ask them to re-form their previous groups and recheck their stacked words for correctness.

Explanation

Students of all ages love game-like activities. This lesson invites them to play a kind of "educated guessing game" while it develops and integrates vocabulary study, questioning, and predicting—all fundamental skills for good readers.

Skill Focus

Asking and answering questions about texts before, during, and after reading; making predictions about texts

Materials & Resources

Text

- Any grade-appropriate fiction or nonfiction text (Used in this lesson: "Building an Igloo," *Click Magazine*, January 1999)

Other

- Photocopies, 1 for each student or student group, of key words from the text

- Scissors

Bonus Ideas

You can also use this method for reviewing commonly missed high-frequency words. Follow the directions in the "Prior to the Lesson" note to create sheets of words. Have students pull apart the word strips and then spread out the strips on their desks. Ask questions about the words and instruct students to answer by selecting words and holding up one or two correct responses. Your questions might focus on word features (beginnings, endings, syllables, vowels, consonants), meanings, antonyms, synonyms—anything you wish to review.

DOORS TO UNDERSTANDING

STEPS

1. Review with students that good readers continually ask questions—both before and throughout their reading. Tell them that in today's lesson they will have a chance to create their own study aid, a little booklet that will help them ask and answer questions.

2. Distribute one sheet of unlined paper and a pair of scissors to each student. Hold up your own sheet and have students follow as you demonstrate how to create the booklet. Fold the paper in half lengthwise. Use a pair of scissors to make four to five horizontal cuts from the right edge to the fold. (See diagram below.)

3. Display the sample text. Model for students how you examine the cover of the book, the title, and the picture. Think aloud as you generate a question based on this information. For the sample text, you might say, "I wonder who the predator is in this book?" Write, "Who is the predator?" on the top tab of your booklet.

4. Now, ask students to think of any question that comes to mind based on the cover and the title. Encourage them to come up with something different from your question. Have them write their questions on the top tab of their booklets.

5. Tell students that as you read aloud the sample text, you will stop briefly after each page or section and ask them to record a question about that material on a booklet tab. They are to listen carefully as you continue reading. When they hear an answer to a question, they should open the tab and write the answer under that opened flap. An example booklet, based on the sample text, is at right.

	There are many different animals—alligators, eagles, and others.
	Do alligators chew their food?
	What are talons?
	How big can barracudas grow?
	What does the polar bear eat?

6. After the reading, invite students who feel they had interesting questions and answers to share those with the class. As well, invite students who didn't find answers to their questions to share their questions. If the question was answered in the text, let other students share the answer and pinpoint the answer's location. If the question was not answered anywhere in the text, open up a discussion with the class.

Mini-Lesson

Three-Part Lesson: Predicting Treasures in Text

Part 1: Make a Bet

Steps

1. Discuss with students that "I bet…" is a common phrase people use when they want to make a guess about something. For instance, they might say, "I bet it's going to rain today." Whenever people use the phrase, they're fairly certain that what they're "betting on" will really happen. Today you'll show students how a good reader might bet, too.

2. Display the transparency of the front page of the I Bet… form (see Appendix, p. 120). Tell students that you'll use this sheet to record your guesses about what will be in the text you're about to read. Read aloud the first unfinished sentence on the I Bet… form: "Looking at the title and cover, I bet.…" Hold up the book or cover page of the text and posit a reasonable bet about its contents. For example, for the sample book, you might say (and fill in on the form), "I bet that the book is about spiders since there's one on the cover. Also, I see that the title has the word *tiny* in it. Since most spiders are considered small, I'm feeling good about my bet."

3. Read aloud the form's next unfinished sentence: "Looking at the big print, I bet.…" Define "big print" for students as chapter titles, headings, and subheadings. Model how you examine these titles and headings. For the sample text, you might observe, "I was feeling good about my bet but now, opening up and turning the pages, I see the big print says, 'Blue Poison Dart Frog.' Hmm, based on the evidence from this feature, I think I'm going to have to make a different bet. Maybe this book is about different tiny animals that are poisonous." Write that in the appropriate place on the form.

4. Read aloud the next part of the I Bet… sheet: "Looking at the pictures and charts, I bet.…" Flip through the pages of the text and make reasonable predictions about its contents. For the sample book, you might say, "Yes, I see pictures of lots of animals. So now I'm even more sure each different section is about a different animal that's small and poisonous. There are also little maps in the corner of each section with an area colored in. I bet that they're telling me where to find each of these animals. I'll write that down."

5. Conclude the modeling by saying something like, "Now I've done a preview of the text and I've placed bets about what I'll be reading."

6. Tell students that it's their turn to place bets about what they'll be reading. Invite them to browse among the texts you have available, or select and distribute a book to each student. Give each student a copy of the form. Instruct them to look at the cover of the text, the big print, and the pictures/charts/illustrations, and then to fill out the front page of the form.

THREE-PART LESSON: PREDICTING TREASURES IN TEXT

PART 2: CHECK THE BET

Explanation

Students need to learn not only to make predictions but to confirm or disprove the predictions as they read. They need to know how to recognize relevant information and use it to evaluate their original guesses. This lesson, the second in a three-part series, models this process for them and then invites them to check their own bets.

Skill Focus

Asking and answering questions about texts before, during, and after reading; making predictions about texts

Materials & Resources

Text

- The same text modeled in Part 1 (Used in this lesson: *Tiny Terrors* by Katharine Kenah)

- The same texts students used in Part 1

Other

- Filled-in transparency from Part 1

- Students' filled-in forms from Part 1

STEPS

1. Display the filled-in transparency from the previous lesson. Tell students that today you're going to check the bets you made in that lesson. To do that you'll need to read the text and see whether each bet was true or false.

2. Read aloud the bet that was based on the text's title and cover. Then read aloud the text until you come to material that confirms or disproves your written bet. Acknowledge your discovery, circle the appropriate notation (either "True" or "False"), and record the page number.

3. Proceed in the same manner for the bet you placed based on the big print, and again for your bet based on the pictures, charts, and illustrations. Be sure students realize that readers usually do all this—making and checking predictions—in their minds as they read. Using the form is just a temporary aid.

4. Explain that good readers are not really concerned if their bets turn out to be incorrect. What's most important is that good readers make these predictions (or place these bets) and then read to confirm or disprove them.

5. Tell students that it's their turn to evaluate their bets. Give them their filled-in copies of the I Bet… form. Make sure students have available the same books they used in Part 1. Instruct them to follow the procedure you have modeled: They should read to a point in the text that confirms or disproves their bet and fill out the form accordingly.

6. Bring the class back together. Invite students to share and discuss their discoveries.

THREE-PART LESSON: PREDICTING TREASURES IN TEXT

PART 3: OVERLOOKED BETS

Explanation

After making predictions and confirming or disproving them, readers can benefit from taking another look to see if there were text or visual clues that should have helped but didn't. Doing so helps readers to sharpen their previewing skills for the future. In this third and final lesson in the series, students have a chance to revisit the same text and to complete the form they've been using.

Skill Focus

Asking and answering questions about texts before, during, and after reading; making predictions about texts

Materials & Resources

Text

- The same text modeled in Parts 1 and 2 (Used in this lesson: *Tiny Terrors* by Katharine Kenah)

- The same texts students used in Parts 1 and 2

Other

- Filled-in transparency from Parts 1 and 2

- Transparency of second side of I Bet... form (Appendix, p. 121)

- Students' 2-sided forms from Parts 1 and 2

Bonus Ideas

Don't forget to use illustrations and graphics to make and confirm your bets. Photographs, charts, drawings, even decorative theme-related page borders or icons can all provide clues for making bets.

STEPS

1. Tell students that good readers aren't able to make predictions or place bets about everything in a text. Say, "It's just not possible to preview everything or to pay attention to every detail that might be important in a text we haven't read yet. In those cases, we hope we will learn the information simply by reading the text and discovering things we never even guessed about. Since it's best to be as thorough as we can, however, in our predictions, today you're going to go back through the text to see what else might have provided a likely basis for a good bet. You're going to figure out why you might have overlooked it. This will help you sharpen your looking and predicting skills for the next time you read."

2. Display the transparency of the reverse side of the I Bet... form (Appendix, p. 121). Begin to read aloud the same text used in Parts 1 and 2. When you encounter an important point about which you'd made no prediction, note that information and write it down on the form under the "Here are new things that I learned:" column. For the sample book, you might write, "An octopus can be extremely small."

3. Now think aloud about whether you should have been able to predict or place bets about these different angles. For the sample text, you might share, "I knew this was an octopus, but I never even thought about how odd it was for an octopus to be in a book on tiny creatures. I could have made a bet that this must be a very small octopus. It turns out this one is only as long as a finger! So, I'll circle 'Yes' since I do think I had enough clues to make a prediction about this." Circle your response and record the appropriate page number on the form.

4. Sum up your modeling by saying something like, "Boys and girls, this is what good readers do. We place bets before we read, confirm or disprove those bets as we read, and then figure out how we might have made even more thorough bets in the first place. All the time, we're gathering treasures—little bits of knowledge that make us more and more informed as readers and thinkers!"

5. Distribute students' forms from Parts 1 and 2 and the same books they used in those previous lessons. Instruct them to follow the procedure you have modeled: They should reread the text to list new information they learned, figure out whether they should have been able to make a prediction about that information before reading, and fill in the form accordingly.

6. Bring the class back together. Invite students to share and discuss their observations.

FIVE-PART LESSON: IS THIS A JUST-RIGHT BOOK?

PART 1: DO I KNOW ANYTHING ABOUT THIS TOPIC?

One of the most important questions a reader can ask is, "Is this book right for me?" To help readers match up with the right books, schools often use a colored-dot system: A particular colored dot on the book's spine indicates a book's readability level. However, students need to move beyond reliance on this system—colored dots won't help them in bookstores, libraries, and in the reading they'll do throughout life. This lesson, the first in a five-part series, will help them learn how to select a just-right book that they can enjoy and understand.

Skill Focus

Asking and answering questions about texts before, during, and after reading; making predictions about texts; asking questions to guide text selections; reading for extended periods of time to derive pleasure and to gain information

Materials & Resources

Text

- 3 books, fiction or nonfiction or an assortment of both, each with a title and cover that clearly define the topic; the books should represent a variety of levels (easy, hard, and just-right) and topics

- A collection of fiction and nonfiction books (about 10 per small group)

Note: *Although these lessons walk your students through the five separate questions in a step-by-step manner, it's important to realize that over time, the questions will become so familiar to students that they will be able to ask several—and eventually all five—at once. Thus, what might appear like a long and even repetitive process here will ultimately be quick and internalized, enabling students to make independent choices.*

STEPS

1. Explain that many readers do not know how to make appropriate book choices. Sometimes students choose books that are too easy and that don't help them grow as readers. Other times they choose books that are so hard they can't understand or enjoy them. When readers make too many inappropriate choices, they no longer like to read. It's just not satisfying! Good readers, though, know how to choose books that are just right for them. They know which key questions to ask themselves. Today you'll share one set of these questions and you'll give each student a tool that will help him or her remember the questions and make the right choices.

2. Display the transparency of the Right Book bookmark. Cover up all but the first question in each column. Explain that the first set of questions all have to do with the bigger question, "Do I know anything about this topic?" Say something like, "Boys and girls, I'm going to pick up a book and ask myself the first question in each of the columns on this bookmark. My answers should help me figure out whether the book will be too easy, too hard, or just right for me to read."

3. From your stack of three sample books, choose one and model your thought process as you work your way through the bookmark questions. For the just-right book in the stack, your think-aloud might sound like this:

> I'm going to start with the first question under the "Just-Right" column since that's the kind of book I hope to find. The directions on the bookmark tell me that every time I answer "yes" in a column, that's a clue that the book might fit in that column. The question is: "Is the book new to you?" My answer is, "Yes, it is." I've seen it before in the library, but I've never looked through it. So that's one clue. Maybe this is a just-right book for me. Let me try the question in the "Too Easy" column. It says, "Have you read it lots of times before?" My answer is, "No, I haven't read it." Finally, I'll look at the first question in the "Too Hard" column, which asks, "Is this an unfamiliar topic?" My answer is, "No, it's not an unfamiliar topic." So, the only column where I

Other

- Photocopies on cardstock, 1 for each student, of the Right Book bookmark (Appendix, p. 119)

- Transparency of the same bookmark (best if enlarged)

- Crayons and markers

⊙ Bonus Ideas

After students have decorated and personalized their bookmarks, it's a good idea to laminate the bookmarks so that they can be used throughout the school year.

answered a definite "yes" was the "Just-Right" column. This might be a just-right book for me!

Go through this same process for the other two books in your stack.

4. Now present each student with a bookmark. Invite them to take a few minutes to personalize their bookmarks. They might draw on the back, write their names, and/or color the top border.

5. Form small groups and provide a stack of books for each group. Instruct students to focus—as you did in the modeling—exclusively on the first row of questions. Within each group, set up partner pairs. One partner should read aloud the first row of questions under each column and the other partner should randomly pick up books from the group's stack until he or she is able to answer "yes" to the question in the "Just-Right" column and "no" to the questions in the other columns. At that point, the questioner should respond, "Then that might be a just-right book for you!" and the two partners should switch roles.

6. Tell students that they'll focus on the next set of "just-right" questions in tomorrow's lesson.

PART 2: DO I UNDERSTAND WHAT I'M READING?

Explanation

One of the most important questions a reader can ask is, "Is this book right for me?" In the previous lesson of this five-part series, students received a tool to help them ask evaluative questions stemming from that overall question, and they focused on the first set of evaluative questions. This lesson picks up from that point and invites them to apply the next set of questions.

Skill Focus

Asking and answering questions about texts before, during, and after reading; making predictions about texts; asking questions to guide text selections; reading for extended periods of time to derive pleasure and to gain information

Materials & Resources

Text

- Same 3 books used in Part 1 for modeling

- Same collection of fiction and nonfiction books used in Part 1

Other

- Right Book bookmark transparency from Part 1

- Students' bookmarks from Part 1

Bonus Ideas

Be sure to keep a Right Book bookmark at your conference table. Start conferences with individual students by asking, "What kind of book did you bring to share with me?" Encourage students to use the new criteria they've learned.

STEPS

1. Challenge students to recall the first big question good readers think about as they're trying to select a just-right book. Guide them as needed to remember that this question, learned in the previous lesson, is "Do I know anything about this topic?" Today you'll share another question that will help them to make wise choices about books they choose.

2. Display the bookmark transparency. Uncover the next row of questions. Explain that the big question for this row is "Do I understand what I'm reading?" Point to the "Just-Right" column and read aloud its question: "Do you understand most of the book?" Say something like, "*Understanding* means that I know what the author has told me. If I can retell what I've just read to myself and it makes sense to me, then I've understood it. I can't just 'call' the words. I really have to know what those words told me. So that's what I'm going to be thinking about today as I ask questions about different books."

3. Call attention to the three sample books you used in the Part 1 lesson. Remind students which one(s) you determined might be just right for you.

4. Pick one of the three and open it to the first text page or pages. Model how you read the beginning sentences or paragraph(s). Pause and say something like, "Now let me stop and see if I understand what I've read," and retell that portion of the text. Ask yourself (and answer) the second-row question in each column. Repeat this process for one or two additional brief text sections. Depending on the book you've picked, your comments will vary. For a too-hard book, you might say, "Yes, I'm confused about what's happening. I'm not getting a lot out of this. Maybe this isn't a just-right book for me." Or for a just-right book, "Yes, I understand most of what I'm reading. I think this is going to be a just-right book for me!" Continue until you've previewed all three books.

5. Form small groups and provide a stack of books for each group. Make sure each student has his or her bookmark available. Instruct students to focus—as you did in the modeling—exclusively on the second row.

6. Within each group, set up partner pairs. One partner should randomly pick up a book from the group's stack. For at least two different times, for approximately two minutes each, he or she should skim the text and then retell what has been read. After each retelling, the other partner should pose the second-row questions. The first partner should continue to pick up books until he or she is able to answer "yes" to the question in the "Just-Right" column and "no" to the questions in the other columns. At that point, the questioner responds, "Then that might be a just-right book for you!" and the two partners switch roles.

FIVE-PART LESSON: IS THIS A JUST-RIGHT BOOK?

PART 3: DO I KNOW MOST OF THE WORDS?

Explanation

This five-part series of lessons continues to examine one of the most important questions a reader can ask: "Is this book right for me?" Students have by now learned to consider questions about their familiarity with a particular book and about their ability to understand what they're reading. This third lesson focuses attention on word-level difficulty.

Skill Focus

Asking and answering questions about texts before, during, and after reading; making predictions about texts; asking questions to guide text selections; reading for extended periods of time to derive pleasure and to gain information

Materials & Resources

Text

- Same 3 books used in Parts 1 and 2 for modeling
- Same collection of fiction and nonfiction books used in Parts 1 and 2

Other

- Right Book bookmark transparency from Part 1
- Students' bookmarks from Part 1

STEPS

1. Review the two questions students learned in the previous two lessons.

2. Display the bookmark transparency. Uncover the third row of questions. Explain that the big question for this row is "Do I know most of the words?" Point to the "Just-Right" column and read aloud: "Are there a few new words?" Tell students that they don't need to know every word in a book to consider it just right. A just-right book should include a few words that are unfamiliar to a reader. That's how we all grow as readers and learn new vocabulary. Too many difficult words, however, will limit a reader's ability to understand the book.

3. Select the most difficult book among your stack of three and attempt to read the first paragraph(s) or page. Model how you struggle with several words. (Be sure to tell students that you're role-playing being a second or third grader!) Refer to the bookmark transparency questions. When you come to the question in the "Too Hard" column—"Are there many hard words?"—respond with a definite "yes." Then exclaim, "I'm confused about what I've just read. Overall, I think there were too many unfamiliar words for me. This wouldn't be a just-right book for me."

4. Now model reading the beginning sentences or paragraph(s) of the sample appropriate book. (Explain again that you'll read it as though you're a second or third grader; this will allow you to miss a word or two.) Stop and report, "If I were in second or third grade, a few of these words would be really big and tough for me. But if I don't find more than a tough word or two on a page and if I still understand what it's saying, then I can answer 'yes' to the bookmark question in the 'Just-Right' column. Remember, that question asks: 'Are there a few new words?' Since I can answer 'yes,' this may be a just-right book for me!"

5. Form small groups and provide a stack of books for each group. Make sure each student has his or her bookmark available. Instruct students to focus—as you did in the modeling—exclusively on the third row of questions.

6. Within each group, set up partner pairs. One partner should randomly pick up a book from the group's stack, read the beginning page or two of the book, and retell what he or she remembers. After the retelling, the reader should count on his or her hands how many words were too difficult to read. No fingers may mean the book is too easy; one or two fingers means the book is probably a just-right book; more than three or four fingers means it is probably too difficult. When the first reader has found a just-right book, partners should switch roles.

FIVE-PART LESSON: IS THIS A JUST-RIGHT BOOK?

PART 4: ARE THERE ONLY A FEW PLACES WHERE MY READING IS CHOPPY?

Explanation

This lesson continues to walk students through the process of selecting a just-right book. As in the previous three lessons in this five-part series, students apply the evaluative questions on their Right Book bookmarks to an assortment of books. This lesson focuses on fluency and stresses that when a reader and a text are well matched, the reading sounds smooth and flows much like regular conversation.

Skill Focus

Asking and answering questions about texts before, during, and after reading; making predictions about texts; asking questions to guide text selections; reading for extended periods of time to derive pleasure and to gain information

Materials & Resources

Text

- Same 3 books used in Parts 1, 2, and 3 for modeling
- Same collection of fiction and nonfiction books used in Parts 1, 2, and 3

Other

- Right Book bookmark transparency
- Students' bookmarks

STEPS

1. Review the three questions students learned in the previous three lessons.

2. Display the bookmark transparency. Uncover the fourth row of questions. Explain that the big question for this row is "Are there only a few places where my reading is choppy?" Point to the "Just-Right" column and read aloud: "When you read, is it mostly smooth?" Say something like, "One of the goals of a good reader is to read the print without having it sound choppy. We want to read the text smoothly—almost the way we talk in our 'everyday lives.'"

3. Pick up the most difficult book from your stack and attempt to read the first paragraph(s) or page. Model reading with a choppy cadence, pausing between words, repeating words, and mispronouncing a few words. (Again, be sure to tell students that you're role-playing being a second or third grader!) Refer to the bookmark transparency questions. When you come to the question in the "Too Hard" column—"When you read, does it sound choppy?"—respond with a definite "yes." Conclude by thinking aloud, "Not only have I responded 'yes' to the 'Too Hard' bookmark question, but I can't really remember much about what I just read. I guess I was concentrating so hard on the difficult words and sentences that I didn't understand the text. Let me keep looking for a just-right book."

4. Now pick up the sample appropriate book. Read this one with fluency—good phrasing and a natural cadence (even though you might model stumbling over a word or two). Refer again to the bookmark questions, this time answering "yes" to the question in the "Just-Right" column. Announce to your students, "I didn't stumble over many words or phrases and I could understand everything I read. This would be a just-right book for me!"

5. Form small groups and provide a stack of books for each group. Make sure each student has his or her bookmark available. Instruct students to focus—as you did in the modeling—exclusively on the fourth row.

6. Within each group, set up partners. One partner should randomly pick up a book from the group's stack and read the beginning page or two of the book. The other partner should pose the relevant bookmark questions. When the first reader has found a just-right book, partners switch roles.

7. Tell students that they'll focus on the final set of "just-right" questions in tomorrow's lesson.

FIVE-PART LESSON: IS THIS A JUST-RIGHT BOOK?

PART 5: DO I THINK WHILE I'M READING THIS BOOK?

Explanation

This final lesson in this five-part series challenges students to consider the last set of questions on the Right Book bookmark. They juxtapose books that are too easy—books that don't make them think enough—with books that are too demanding. Finally, they experience a book with a just-right concept load. At the conclusion of this lesson series, students retain their personal bookmarks for use in evaluating books throughout the year.

Skill Focus

Asking and answering questions about texts before, during, and after reading; making predictions about texts; asking questions to guide text selections; reading for extended periods of time to derive pleasure and to gain information

Materials & Resources

Text

- Same 3 books used in Parts 1, 2, 3, and 4 for modeling

- Same collection of fiction and nonfiction books used in Parts 1, 2, 3, and 4

Other

- Right Book bookmark transparency

- Students' bookmarks

Bonus Ideas

Listen for comments and reflections students might make about their reading. When that special remark comes along, find a space on your board and write "thin<u>KING</u>." Write the student's name and praise him or her for demonstrating royal reading habits!

STEPS

1. Review the four questions students learned in the previous lessons.

2. Display the bookmark transparency. Uncover the final row of questions. Explain that the big question for this row is "Do I think while I'm reading this book?" Point to the "Just-Right" column and read aloud its question: "Do you have to think as you read?" Explain that good readers need to be active thinkers while they read. Say something like, "If I'm reading without even having to think, the book is definitely too easy. I know that a just-right book will make me think. Reading is all about thinking! But, if I have to think too much, I probably won't enjoy the book and it won't be right for me. So there's a balance that I'm looking for."

3. Pick up the easiest book from your stack. Model reading the beginning page or two with total fluency. Refer to the bookmark transparency questions. When you come to the question in the "Too Easy" column— "Are you reading without thinking?"—respond with a definite "yes." Comment, "That was so easy for me! I really didn't have to stop and think about it to understand it. Let me find something that's more challenging."

4. Now hold up the most difficult book. Tell students you'll read it as if you were in second or third grade. Stop after every sentence or two to say, "Let me see—what did I just read?" Model struggling to make sense of the book. Refer to the bookmark transparency questions. When you come to the question in the "Too Hard" column—"Do you find you're not enjoying this book?"—respond with a definite "yes." Add, "I have to think too hard with this book! Let me see if I can find something else that might be just right."

5. Next, pick up the sample appropriate book. Read it with fluency, hesitating only occasionally. Refer again to the bookmark questions, this time answering "yes" to the question in the "Just-Right" column.

6. Form small groups and provide a stack of books for each group. Make sure each student has his or her bookmark available. Instruct students to focus—as you did in the modeling—exclusively on the fifth row.

7. Within each group, set up partner pairs. One partner should randomly pick up a book from the group's stack and read the beginning page or two of the book. The other partner should pose the relevant bookmark questions. When the first reader has found a just-right book, partners should switch roles.

8. Remind students that their Right Book bookmarks are theirs to keep—and to use often!—throughout the school year.

TWO-PART LESSON: APPLYING QUESTION WORDS TO NARRATIVE TEXT

PART 1: USING THE QUESTIONS TO FIND BIG IDEAS

···○ Explanation

This two-part lesson series provides students with a new way to examine narrative text: They learn to apply the key news reporting questions (the 5 Ws and the H) to fiction. Becoming familiar with these Question Words will help students in several different ways—locating specific information, understanding narrative elements, and preparing for test taking.

···○ Skill Focus

Asking and answering questions about texts before, during, and after reading; responding to questions of *who, what, why, when, where,* and *how*; questioning to clarify reading

···○ Materials & Resources

Text

- A narrative text such as a familiar folktale or fairy tale, or a short story that is either new or familiar to students (Used in this lesson: "Cinderella")

Other

- Transparency or chalkboard

···○ Bonus Ideas

Challenge students to read a new short story and locate the answers to the 5 Ws and the H. Have students work in small cooperative groups. Each group should designate one student to be the recorder. The recorder traces his or her hand on a sheet of paper and then assigns each group member to be in charge of one W question (or two, for setting) or the H question. The designated person is responsible for that particular question's being answered on the traced handprint.

STEPS

1. Trace your hand on a transparency or the chalkboard. On the tips of the fingers write the words *Who?, What?, Why?, When?* and *Where?* (together on one fingertip), and *How?* Explain that readers can use these six Question Word questions—which news reporters and other writers often call the 5Ws and the H—as a way to locate key information and to summarize most narrative texts.

2. On the board or at the bottom of the transparency, write the Question Words and brief definitions as shown below:

Question Words	
Who?	This is the main character—the person at the center of most of the action in the story.
What?	This is the problem in the story—what happens to the character?
Why?	Why is what happened a problem?
When? and	This is the part of the setting that tells when the story takes place—for example, past/present/future, day/night, spring/summer/fall/winter.
Where?	This is the part of the setting that tells where the story takes place—for example, in the kitchen, on a beach, in New York, on a hillside.
How?	How is the problem resolved and how does the story end?

3. Read the sample text aloud. Call attention to the drawing of your hand. Invite students to help you fill in the answers in the appropriate locations on the drawing.

4. Tell students that tomorrow will be their turn to use their hands as graphic organizers and answer the 5 Ws and the H!

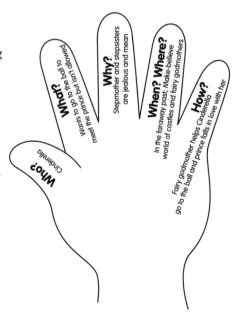

TWO-PART LESSON: APPLYING QUESTION WORDS TO NARRATIVE TEXT

PART 2: USING THE QUESTION WORDS TO FIND DETAILS

Explanation

Now that students are familiar with the six Question Words and have learned to apply them to narrative texts, they can focus on looking for details or clues to support and enhance their responses. This lesson begins what you can use as a full series of lessons, each of which examines one of the Question Words. In the end, students will have five hand outlines, expressing everything they need to know about a particular story!

Skill Focus

Asking and answering questions about texts before, during, and after reading; responding to questions of *who, what, why, when, where,* and *how*; questioning to clarify reading

Materials & Resources

Text

- A narrative text such as a familiar folktale or fairy tale, or a story that is either new or familiar to students (Used in this lesson: *Mr. George Baker* by Amy Hest)

Other

- Transparency or chalkboard
- Sticky notes cut into strips
- Sheet of unlined paper, 1 for each student

Bonus Ideas

The 5Ws and the H are typically used in journalistic writing. Have students underline the information that answers the Question Words in a newspaper article. Note how concisely these questions are handled and compare this to the way they unfold in a narrative.

Note: This lesson focuses only on the first of the six Question Words. You can use the same procedure on subsequent days for each of the remaining questions.

STEPS

1. Briefly discuss the six Question Words students learned in the previous lesson—the 5 Ws and the H—and review how these questions can be applied to narrative text. Tell students that today they'll explore in greater depth the nature of these important questions and they'll learn to locate text clues to help them arrive at thorough, informative answers.

2. Display the sample text and read it through once, just for enjoyment. Then tell students that as you read it aloud a second time, you'll be looking for answers to each of the Question Words.

3. Trace your handprint on a transparency or the chalkboard. In the palm of the hand, write "Who?" Remind students that this question asks you about the main character. So, as you read, you're going to look for things that tell what the character looks like and what the character does.

4. Begin to read the story for the second time. Each time you locate a clue, tear off a sticky note strip and place it next to the clue. Proceed this way until you reach a total of five clues. For the sample story, you might note:

   - He's 100 years old.
   - He never learned to read.
   - He's kind—he jokes with the little boy.
   - He's a famous drummer.
   - He goes to school.

5. After noting several clues, return to the handprint. On the palm, under the "Who?" question, write the name of the character. On each of the fingers, jot down a clue. Read back over the clues on the handprint and summarize what you've learned about this character. Then write a summary sentence in the palm to answer the "Who?" question with details from the fingers. For the sample text, you might write, "Mr. Baker is a talented, kind gentleman who wants to learn to read at age 100!"

6. Distribute a sheet of unlined paper to each student. Have students trace their hands, following your model, and write the question "Who?" in the palm.

7. In their independent or assigned reading today, have students read a new text and hunt for details about the character. Using their own handprint outlines, they should write one clue on each finger and then summarize their findings.

POINT OR PONDER QUESTIONS AND ANSWERS

Explanation

Differentiating between literal and implied information is an essential reading skill. It's especially important when readers are asked to locate information in text. In these instances, knowing whether the information is explicitly stated or whether it's implied permits the reader to search and respond more effectively. This lesson gives students practice in making these key differentiations.

Skill Focus

Asking and answering questions about texts before, during, and after reading; responding to questions of *who*, *what*, *why*, *when*, *where*, and *how*; questioning to clarify reading

Materials & Resources

Text

- Any grade-appropriate text, fiction or nonfiction (Used in this lesson: *Mr. George Baker* by Amy Hest)

Bonus Ideas

For further practice, you might pair students. Using the same text or a different familiar book, have students make up questions about the text, ask their partner to decide whether it's a "point" or "ponder," and then provide the answer. After a few questions, have partners switch roles.

STEPS

1. Tell students that there are two broad types of answers to questions about text they're reading. On the board or a transparency, draw a finger. Explain that some answers to questions can be pointed to in text. Today, you'll call those answers "point answers."

2. Display the sample book. (If you used this book in the previous lesson, it will already be familiar to students. If not, read the book aloud.) Pose several literal questions based on this book and then demonstrate how you find "point answers" to these questions. Several questions and answers, all of which are stated directly in the text, follow.

How old is George Baker?	"He's a 100 years old, no kidding."
Where is he learning to read?	"See this man, this one in Room 7? He's learning to read."
Who comes out of the house?	"You know who teeters out of the house? Mrs. Baker."

3. Now explain that the second type of answer can't be found by pointing to the text. Readers must construct these answers by putting text clues together and figuring things out. These are the answers readers must ponder, so today you'll call them "ponder answers." On the board or a transparency, sketch a profile of a head with the outline of a brain inside.

4. Call attention again to the sample text. Pose several inferential questions based on this book and then demonstrate how you use text clues to figure out "ponder answers" to these questions. Below is a list of several questions and answers, all of which must be figured out from text clues. (The text clues themselves are provided within parentheses.)

Why is George learning to read?	He seems to think it's something that he just needs to know how to do.
What does Henry think of Mr. Baker?	He seems to adore him. (He loves Mr. Baker's clothes. He wants to sit beside him on the bus every day.)
Is George happily married?	He seems to love his wife very much. (His wife kisses him when she brings him his lunch, and he gets up and dances with her.)

5. Continue by flipping through the sample book and posing several additional questions about the text. Challenge the class to decide whether the answers to these questions are "point" or "ponder." Direct students to hold up their index (or pointer) finger if they think the answer is a point answer. Direct them to scratch their heads (as thinkers do!) if they feel the answer is one that must be pondered.

Using Graphic and Semantic Organizers

Graphic and semantic organizers—diagrams or pictorial representations that visually illustrate concepts and relationships—play an essential role in building students' reading comprehension. Adaptable for use with just about any kind of fiction or nonfiction text, they make vague and abstract ideas concrete so that students can more easily process and understand these concepts.

The National Reading Panel reports that these tools have a positive impact on three specific areas of learning:

1. They help students focus on text structure while reading.

2. They provide a framework that visually represents textual relationships.

3. They facilitate students' ability to write well-organized summaries. (NRPR; NICHHD, 2000)

The National Reading Panel research also says that "teaching students to use a systematic, visual graphic to organize the ideas that they are reading about develops the ability of the students to remember what they read and may transfer in general to better comprehension and achievement in social studies and science content areas" (NRPR; NICHHD, p. 4-75).

For this author, and others in past generations, the closest experience to using true graphic organizers was the venerable exercise of diagramming sentences. The sentence diagram (which offered a means of picturing the technical aspects of sentence construction) can even be seen as a precursor to today's graphic organizers. Many students may have huffed and grunted, "Why are we doing this?" but in the end, relationships among sentence parts were distilled and represented in a uniquely clear way. Some of us may hate to admit it, but we actually enjoyed this puzzle of lines! We are not advocating going back to sentence-diagramming days, but realizing the strengths of this approach can help us better grasp the valuable role of all graphics in literacy instruction. Indeed, such graphics can be the key for some students—especially those who are visual learners—in achieving comprehension of many abstract concepts.

Although there are countless versions of organizers available, the research of Bromley, Irwin-De Vitis, and Modlo (1995) suggests that there are four basic structures from which all graphic and semantic organizers evolve: conceptual, sequential, hierarchical, and cyclical. In the lessons in this section, you will find examples of all four structures. Students are given opportunities to work with and create a myriad of different kinds of maps and organizers. For example, using the familiar concept of a family tree, they learn to map out hierarchical relationships among

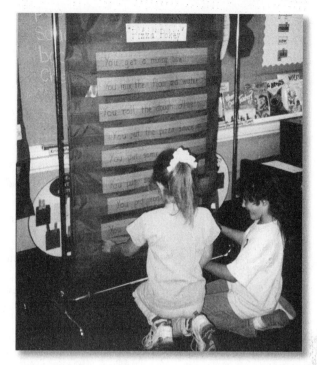

A full-sized sequential organizer is a great way for students to demonstrate their knowledge of correct sequence.

This semantic organizer provides a place for students to draw the clues that will help them formulate a main idea.

concepts in a science text, or, expanding their understanding of cycles from the fun Laura Numeroff books, they create cyclical maps to represent stages and steps within content area texts. They track changes within characters' personalities in narrative text, cluster vocabulary terms within concept circles, map story elements, and much more! Have fun with your students as you engage in learning through graphic and semantic organizers.

USING HIERARCHICAL MAPS

Explanation

By second and third grade, most students already realize that conceptual and text information can be represented visually. However, they may be familiar with only one or two simple models, such as concept webs. Now is the time to expand their repertoire. This lesson introduces them to the essential organizational pattern of hierarchy—and gives them a chance to think about their own position on the family tree hierarchy at the same time!

Skill Focus

Organizing and categorizing information; developing vocabulary through concrete experiences

Materials & Resources

Text

- Any grade-appropriate informational or content area text with a hierarchical text organization (Used in this lesson: chapter on oceans in Harcourt Science)

- Additional informational texts with text organized in a hierarchical pattern

Other

- Blank transparencies (or chalkboard)

- Index cards (8 or 9 cards for each small group)

- Transparency of topic map/ concept web (optional)

Prior to the Lesson: You'll need to go through the texts that students use (see Step 5) and identify the key words for each.

STEPS

1. Review with students that many graphic organizers can be randomly filled in—that is, they do not represent ideas in any particular order. To help students recall these kinds of organizers, discuss and/or display an example of a simple topic map or concept web. (Most students have worked with these kinds of organizers since kindergarten or first grade.) For instance, you might describe or display a topic map about summer. Remind students that this kind of map simply has the main word in a center circle, with spokes radiating out to words like *hot, swim, vacation, shorts, barefoot, beach,* and *camp.* Stress that although the words must all be placed around the central main idea, the order of the words on the spokes doesn't matter at all.

2. Now explain that there is a type of graphic organizer that represents information in a specific way. Write the word *hierarchy* on the board. Tell students that a hierarchy is like a ladder on which all the rungs flow downward from the top. To help students better visualize this kind of organizer, provide a familiar example such as a family tree. Explain that in a family tree, the top box represents the origin or beginning; all the other boxes flow out of that first one. On the board or a transparency, you might sketch something like the following:

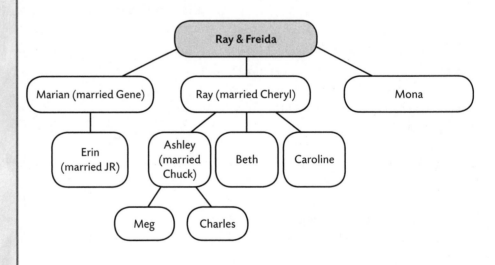

3. Tell students that text information can be organized in a hierarchical pattern much like a family tree. Read aloud the sample text.

4. Using a transparency or the board, sketch out a hierarchical map of the text. As you fill in the boxes, explain to students that this kind of mapping reflects how the main topic flows down to the smaller details. An example follows:

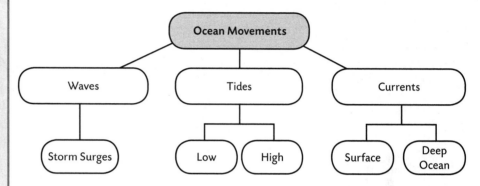

5. Organize students into small groups. Distribute selected informational books and a set of index cards to each group. On the board or a transparency, list key words for each text. Have students copy one key word onto each index card.

6. Have each group read the text. After reading, invite the groups to arrange the cards to create a hierarchical formation that reflects how the main topic flows down to the smaller details. When the groups are finished, have them share their work with the whole class.

USING SEQUENTIAL STORY MAPS

Explanation

A story map is a simple way to remind students of the basic building blocks of narrative text. Once students have practiced using a story map several times, they'll develop a greater understanding of these elements and they'll learn to look for them in all stories. In addition, the story map used in this lesson helps students focus on sequence as they learn to list in order the events that occur within one key story element—plot.

Skill Focus

Organizing and categorizing information; developing vocabulary through concrete experiences

Materials & Resources

Text

- A narrative text (Used in this lesson: *Wolf* by Becky Bloom)

Other

- Transparency of Story Map (see Appendix, p. 122)

STEPS

1. Remind students that all stories are made up of similar parts called "elements." Display the Story Map transparency and review the elements. As you discuss each element, sketch something simple to remind students about the meaning of that literary term. For example, for the term "Characters," you might draw a stick figure of a person. (At the same time, remind students that a story's characters—even the main character—do not have to be people. They might be animals or fanciful creatures.) For "Setting," you might sketch a simple house or forest. For "Problem" you could depict a lightning bolt, and for "Solution," you could put a strike through the bolt or perhaps draw a smiley face. "Plot" could be represented by a simple outline of ascending steps. Finally, for "Ending," you might include a bow to convey the idea that events have been tied up by the story's conclusion. Tell students that these visual symbols can serve to aid them in remembering and identifying the elements.

2. Read aloud the model story one time just for students' enjoyment. Tell the class to pay special attention to the elements you've just discussed to see if they can recognize them as they listen to the story.

3. Now read the story aloud a second time. Ask students to raise their hands as soon as they can identify a character. Add that character's name to the story map.

4. Follow this same process for identifying the other elements, and add them to the story map. Explain that for "Plot," as the chart format indicates, students are to identify specific important plot events in the order—or the sequence—in which they occur. A completed Story Map for the sample book might look like this:

Story Map

Characters		**Main:** Wolf **Other:** Pig, Duck, Cow
Setting		Outside on a farm
Problem		Wolf couldn't read.
PLOT	Event	Wolf was hungry and was going to eat the farm animals.
	Event	The animals were busy reading and told him to go away.
	Event	He decided to learn to read.
	Event	His first reading was too slow.
	Event	His next reading was too fast.
Solution		Soon he learned to read just right and the animals wanted to listen.
Ending		They all became good friends.

5. Conclude the lesson by inviting different volunteers to list the six elements and to define them. Remind students to look out for these story parts in all the narrative texts they read.

COMPARING TEXTS OR TEXT ELEMENTS

Explanation

The venerable Venn diagram is certainly one effective way to represent comparisons within, between, and among texts. However, not only is it overused—it may not always be the most appropriate choice. This lesson provides a variation that may be easier for young students to use and to visualize.

Skill Focus

Organizing and categorizing information; developing vocabulary through concrete experiences

Materials & Resources

Text

- Any grade-appropriate fiction or nonfiction text with elements that can be compared (Used in this lesson: *The Wednesday Surprise* by Eve Bunting and *Mr. George Baker* by Amy Hest)

- Several paired grade-appropriate texts for student work

Other

- Transparency of Text Comparison Chart (see Appendix, p. 122)

- Photocopies, 1 per student, of same chart

Bonus Ideas

Challenge students to compare a designated element(s) within three different text selections. You can use the same Text Comparison Chart template but add an additional unshaded column. Remind students that the shaded column should include only characteristics shared among all three texts.

STEPS

1. Review with students what it means to compare two or more items. Guide students to realize that making comparisons can be a means to greater understanding: By looking at something as it compares to something else, we can better see the unique characteristics of each. For readers this means that comparing one text to another can provide greater insight into each selection. During or after reading a new story, good readers frequently recall other stories they've read. They wonder, "What do these stories have in common? How is this new one different from other(s) I've read?"

2. Display your selected texts. Tell students you want them to pay extra careful attention to the characters in the two stories. Read both stories to or with your students. (Note: If your selected texts are too long for one sitting, you might want to read one or both a day ahead of this lesson.)

3. Display the transparency of the Text Comparison Chart (see Appendix, p. 122). Elicit students' help as you compare one or more elements in the two stories. Fill in the chart, making sure to point out to students that the shaded middle column is intended for only those characteristics shared by both texts, while the two outer columns are for characteristics unique to each text. A completed chart that compares the two main characters in the sample books follows:

Story Element of *Main Character* in Text # 1 (*Mr. Baker*)	How They Are Similar	Story Element of *Main Character* in Text # 2 (*Grandma*)
He is 100 years old. He is a drummer. He goes to school. He is married.	Both are old. Both don't know to read. Both learn to read. Both have someone help them. Both have young friends who admire them.	She is an older person, but not 100. She wants to read everything after learning how to read. Her granddaughter teaches her on Wednesdays. We don't know if she has a husband.

4. Organize students into small groups. Distribute a pair of brief stories or text selections to each group (each text pair should share elements that can be easily compared). Distribute photocopies of the Text Comparison Chart.

5. Have groups read their texts. After reading, students in each group should work together to fill out the charts. (You might choose to have each student fill out his or her own chart with the group's agreed-upon information or you might suggest groups select a scribe who fills in one group chart.) When the groups are finished, have them share their work with the whole class.

TRACKING CHARACTERS' CHANGES

Explanation

Students need to be aware that characters in narrative text often change as a story unfolds from the beginning to the conclusion. This lesson provides students with several concrete ways to understand and track those transformations.

Skill Focus

Organizing and categorizing information; developing vocabulary through concrete experiences; identifying characters in literary works; analyzing characters

Materials & Resources

Text

- Multiple copies of a narrative text in which the main character changes (Used in this lesson: *Swimmy* by Leo Lionni)

Other

- 1 sticky note for each student snipped into VIP strips

STEPS

1. Explain to students that stories are almost always about change. Often the change occurs within or to a character. Good readers are observant, always watching out for these changes because they realize the changes usually reveal a great deal about the story's meaning. They observe the story's characters carefully, from the very beginning through the middle to the story's end because the changes may occur at any point, or all through the story line.

2. To help students grasp these concepts more deeply, review several fairy tales or recent stories the class has read. On a transparency or the board, draw a simple four-column grid. In the left hand column, fill in the titles and the main characters of the fairy tales or familiar stories. At the top of the other three columns, write "Beginning," "Middle," and "End." Work with students to identify how the character felt in the beginning of the story and draw a face that represents this feeling in the appropriate column. Continue in this way until the chart is completed. One example, based on two fairy tales, follows:

	Beginning	Middle	End
Cinderella (from "Cinderella")	☹	☺ ☹	☺
Hansel and Gretel (from "Hansel and Gretel")	☺ ☺	☹ ☹	☺ ☺

3. Distribute a sticky note cut into VIP strips to each student. Have students pull the "fingers" apart so that each student has several separate, narrow strips.

4. Now distribute copies of the selected text to students. Tell the class that you're going to read this story aloud as they read along with you. Their job is to pay attention to the whole story and to look especially for changes that happen to the main character.

5. For example, on the first page of the sample book *Swimmy* happily spends time with his friends in the ocean. After reading to the end of this page (which has only one paragraph of text), ask students to stop and place a sticky finger on the page and to draw a face that expresses Swimmy's feelings. (Students will likely draw a smiling face.) In the second

Bonus Ideas

To follow up this lesson, have students further analyze the development of a character they've read about. Using a chart like the one shown below, they should first draw in faces to depict the character's evolution. Next they should jot down text clues that support their evaluations.

Story	Character's Feelings	Clues
Beginning		
Middle		
End		

paragraph, still the beginning of the story, everything changes. All of Swimmy's friends are devoured by a large fish, and he finds himself alone, scared, and sad. Stop again. Have students place a sticky finger on the page and draw a representative expression.

6. Continue reading until you come to the middle of the story. In the sample book, Swimmy explores the ocean alone and discovers many wonders in its depths. Alert students to the fact that often (but not always) characters experience a change in the middle of a story. Stop at a few spots in the middle and invite students to place another sticky finger on the page that most clearly shows how Swimmy now feels. They will likely change his frowning face into a neutral or smiling face.

7. Finish reading the story. At the end, discuss how Swimmy has changed. He has now found new friends and has helped them figure out how to protect themselves from the fate of his first group of friends. Have students place a final sticky finger on the last page. (This should be a smiling face.)

8. Return to the four-column grid you and the class have already created. Add a row for the story you have just read. Invite students to come forward to help you draw in the appropriate faces that depict how the character changed throughout the story. (See diagram below.)

	Beginning	Middle	End
Cinderella (from "Cinderella")	☹	☺ ☹	☺
Hansel and Gretel (from "Hansel and Gretel")	☺ ☺	☹ ☹	☺ ☺
Swimmy (from *Swimmy*)	☺ ☹	😐	☺

9. Conclude the lesson by emphasizing that good readers must always be on the lookout to see if, how, and when characters change as stories progress.

Using Cyclical Maps

Explanation

Cyclic graphic organizers represent a particular kind of logical order that students need to work with and understand. Science text provides many rich contexts for such organizers: food chains, water cycles, erosion, and life cycles, among others. This lesson demonstrates this fundamental concept while at the same time tapping your students' artistic talents and their written communication skills.

Skill Focus

Organizing and categorizing information; developing vocabulary through concrete experiences; using logical order

Materials & Resources

Text

- Nonfiction text selection that includes cyclic information: 1 copy for teacher and 1 for each partner pair (Used in this lesson: Subsection, "Processes that Cause Change," in the chapter, "How Rocks Change" in *Earth Science*, Harcourt Science)

- *If You Give a Mouse a Cookie* or *If You Give a Moose a Muffin,* or similar cyclic book by Laura Numeroff

Other

- 1 sticky note, snipped into VIP strips, for each partner pair
- Unlined paper (1 sheet for each step of the process being mapped)
- Tape
- Crayons or markers
- Clothes hanger

Steps

1. Tell students that today they will learn about events that happen in *cycles*—that is, that occur predictably one after the other until the final event usually leads right back to the starting event. To help students understand the concept of cycle better, and to have some fun at the same time, you might read aloud a children's book like *If You Give a Mouse a Cookie* by Laura Numeroff, which provides a simple illustration of events that occur in cycles.

2. Next, read aloud the selected text section that you'll use for mapping. For example, in the sample text you'll read about how rocks begin as one type, undergo many changes over the course of thousands of years, and then often return to their original state.

3. Organize the class into partners. Distribute a copy of the selection and a sticky note cut into VIP strips to each partner pair. Have students reread the selection. At each spot in the text that describes a different rock transformation stage, they should place a VIP strip and number it appropriately.

4. Bring the whole class together to check and review the stages students have noted. On a transparency or the board, write the stages as a numbered list. For the sample text, the list might look like this:

   1) Basalt, the most common igneous rock, is formed when lava cools.
   2) The basalt is broken into small pieces by tree roots, freezing, and thawing.
   3) Wind and rain carry the small pieces to the river where the edges are rounded off.
   4) Rounded pieces become sediment on the bottom.
   5) The sediment gets squeezed and compacted, becoming sedimentary rock.
   6) Heat and pressure change it into metamorphic rock.
   7) Metamorphic rock melts, cools, and becomes igneous rock again.

5. Divide the class into small groups—one group for each step or stage in the cycle. Give each group an unlined sheet of paper and assign them a step. Each group's job is to illustrate and write a brief description of their step. Have all groups orient their sheets the same way—either vertically or horizontally.

6. Collect all sheets and tape them together, in logical order, with the last section taped to the first to form a loop. (Depending upon the orientation of the sheets, you'll tape them at the tops and bottoms or at the sides.) Before you tape the last section to the first, insert a clothes hanger. This will make it easy to hang and display your class's unique cycle!

USING CONCEPT MAPS

Prior to the Lesson: Go through the selected text and identify two or three core concepts or characters. Then cull and list key phrases, vocabulary words, and/or facts that pertain to the core concepts or characters. For example, in a narrative text that includes several different characters, you might list the characters' names and all their traits; for a chapter about weather in a science text, you might list terms for different types of clouds and all their characteristics. (To provide an additional challenge, you might also list a few phrases or facts that don't pertain to the two or three core concepts.)

STEPS

1. Explain to students that today they are going to work with clusters—that is, groups of words and concepts that cluster together to describe a big idea or a story character. By placing related words and phrases in cluster graphics, they'll have a chance to think more deeply about the relationships and to recall the information in a more organized fashion.

2. On a transparency or the board, list in random order the phrases or words that match up with the two or three core concepts or characters to be explored. List, as well, the additional terms that do not pertain to the core concepts/characters. For example, for the sample text, you might identify two major concepts—alligators' physical characteristics and habitats of alligators—and list terms that fit one or the other of these categories. As a challenge, you might also include terms that relate to crocodiles. A model scrambled list for the sample book is shown below (for your convenience, information about crocodiles is asterisked).

- eyes high on head
- hold breath one hour
- long scaly tails
- 200 million years old *
- Eastern China
- SE United States
- deep holes
- lower teeth show *
- broad rounded noses
- longer skinnier noses *
- short stubby legs
- salt water *
- lower teeth don't show
- fresh water
- 80 sharp teeth
- crankier, bolder, fiercer *
- live 50 years
- lay eggs
- live in ponds, lakes, swamps, marshes
- Spanish word for lizard *
- ancient *
- Florida

a key word (either a content area word or an interesting new vocabulary word). Invite students to come forward on their own over a period of time to write related words within the circle. These might be synonyms or simply words that are associated with the core term. Students might locate the words in their independent or assigned reading or from lists that you provide. Call the class's attention to the circle when it is full and hold a discussion about the clustered words.

3. Distribute a sheet of unlined paper to each student. Instruct students to draw a circle for each character or core concept and to label their circles appropriately.

4. Next, invite students to read through the list of traits or facts and to decide if they think they might know ahead of hearing the text where some of these cluster. If so, have them jot down those traits or facts in the circles. Be sure they use pencils as they may wind up discovering that some of their assumptions turn out to be incorrect!

5. Read aloud the whole text selection. Then read it a second time, pausing occasionally so that students can write (or reposition) the list words in the correct circles on their sheets of paper.

6. Draw the appropriate number of circles on the board. Have volunteers come forward to the board (or to write on the transparency) to fill in the circles. As a class, discuss and resolve any differences of opinion. A set of completed circles for the sample text, based on the list in Step 2, follows:

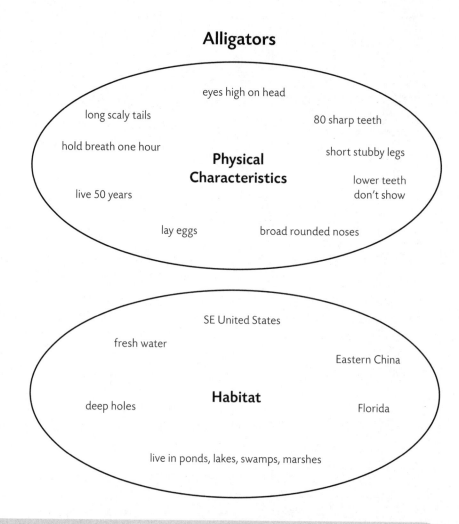

Alligators

Physical Characteristics

eyes high on head
long scaly tails
80 sharp teeth
hold breath one hour
short stubby legs
lower teeth don't show
live 50 years
lay eggs
broad rounded noses

Habitat

SE United States
fresh water
Eastern China
deep holes
Florida
live in ponds, lakes, swamps, marshes

Creating and Using Images

Almost every one of us has been sorely disappointed by the movie version of a favorite book. As good readers, we've not only read that book, we've visualized every scene and character. In a sense, we've already seen the play or movie in our mind's eye. We've held our own casting of characters, sometimes using people we know or stars we admire. We've already used our own props to establish the setting; we've called on numerous personal experiences and preferences to enrich our understanding of the plot. Then, we see what a Hollywood producer has envisioned for us—and so often it just doesn't match. And, not surprisingly, we like our version better! Most likely, without even consciously realizing it, we've been making use of a sophisticated, essential reading skill—the ability to form images based in part on connections we've made between our own experiences and the text we're reading.

This ability not only makes reading more enjoyable, it enables readers to grow as learners. The research of Gambrell and Koskinen (2002) suggests that there are two great advantages to creating and using mental images when reading: 1) Images provide a framework, or "pegs," for organizing and remembering information from texts; and 2) mental images help integrate information across texts. To further understand the importance of visualizing while reading, let's take a look inside a primary-grade classroom.

As a teacher reads *Our Living Forests* by Allan Fowler, children around the room are processing what is heard in many different ways. Two of them—Tricia and Henry—have very little personal knowledge of forests. They live in a suburban town with plantings limited to parks and gardens, and neither student has traveled widely. Tricia, however, has an advantage: She knows how to use the descriptive words in the text to conjure up a reasonable picture of what those places she's hearing about probably look like. Henry listens to *Our Living Forests* intently. He hears the words and he knows individually what they all mean, but he doesn't see pictures as the words are read. He isn't even aware that good readers form pictures in their minds as they read. As a result, Tricia winds up learning new things from this book and extending her knowledge, while Henry gets stuck early on and loses out on an important learning experience.

One of the greatest challenges teachers face in enabling students to create mental images is addressing gaps in prior experiences. But the problem is greatly compounded when children also lack skills and experience in using language to make connections and generate mind pictures. Certainly, both Tricia and Henry can benefit from gaining background knowledge about forests—perhaps through downloaded Internet photos, classroom textbook illustrations, or class discussion involving students who know firsthand about forests. But for Tricia, who already has a profound learning tool available, these instructional experiences will play a different, less fundamental role than for Henry. Like many good readers, from the moment she hears a book's title, she begins to create mental images. And throughout her reading (or listening), Tricia is able to use her knowledge of language to make connections—for example, through analogies or similes—and conjure up images of something she has never seen in real life.

Learning to integrate information from images with text information is a key reading skill.

For students like Henry, however, for whom language, imaging skills, and background experiences are all limited, the teacher's job is more difficult. She must provide not only pictures to help him form a knowledge base, but also experience with the language that's related to those pictures before Henry can really make use of them. This can be a time-consuming and challenging task for a teacher, but the impact on the student can be great and the effort can definitely pay off.

The lessons in this section are aimed at helping teachers help students like Henry develop key imaging skills (and, at the same time, reinforce these skills for students like Tricia). Imagery training has long proven successful as a way to improve students' memory and inferential reasoning about written text (Levin and Divine-Hawkins, 1974; Borduin, Borduin, and Manley, 1994). You'll find lessons here on many different aspects of visualizing—from telling stories through illustrations to interpreting nonfiction graphics to highlighting figurative language. So, as we begin this section, let your "good reader" camera roll. We believe you'll gain some unique ideas for teaching your students to see what they read so that they can better comprehend it.

THE MOVIES IN YOUR MIND

Explanation

Creating mind pictures as we read—and revising them as we read further and discover new information—are essential reading skills. However, for some students, the ability to visualize doesn't come automatically: They don't see the "picture show" in their minds that good readers need to be able to see. This lesson models for students how to do just that. At the same time, it encourages students to revise their images as they find more clues.

Skill Focus

Creating mental images when reading; using graphics such as charts, pictures, and graphic organizers as information sources and as a means of organizing information logically

Materials & Resources

Text

- Any grade-appropriate text for modeling (Used in this lesson: *Fire on the Mountain* by Jane Kurtz)

- Assortment of grade-appropriate texts for students

STEPS

1. Discuss with students how good readers actually "watch" the story that they're reading. Explain that when you read a good book, a story, or even informational text, it can be like going to the movies—only the movie takes place in your mind. For example, when good readers meet characters in a book, they imagine how the characters look. This is such an important part of reading that when readers do not form mental images during reading, their comprehension suffers.

2. Continue by pointing out that readers also need to revise and modify their images when they find new text clues. Otherwise, they might be seeing something very different from what the author intended and their comprehension will be affected.

3. Using your selected text, model the process you use to visualize. As you read, pause occasionally to think aloud about what you're picturing in your mind. Be sure to include images that need to be revised once additional text is read. An example think-aloud, based on the sample text, follows:

What the Text Says	Your Think-Aloud
While he was watching the cows, he also watched the rich man as he rode by.	"I'm picturing a man in fancy clothes riding by in a big, shiny car while Alemaya is in the pasture."
He rode on his mule with a man carrying an umbrella walking behind him.	"I've got to change the picture in my mind. I need to remember that this is happening in Ethiopia long ago. Now I'm picturing two men—the rich man on a mule with another man following him with a big umbrella. I've never seen anything like that myself but I can use the author's words to imagine it."
The rich man says, "But you must take nothing to keep you warm but one thin shemma."	"I'm having a hard time picturing this because I don't know what a shemma is. Since the text says, 'to keep you warm,' I'll just picture a jacket until I get more clues."

4. After the modeling, tell students you're now going to give them a chance to do the visualizing. Continue reading the same text. Pause at likely spots and call on volunteers to describe what pictures they're seeing in their minds. Do this until you feel students seem comfortable with the process.

5. Set up partners. Using either an assigned or independent text, one partner should read aloud and stop at certain intervals to tell the other student what he is picturing in his mind. The listeners can comment on whether they have pictured the same image. After several pages, partners should switch roles. Be sure students realize that variations in readers' mind pictures are natural. We rely on our experiences to paint these pictures, and we all have had different experiences in life.

PICTURE RIDDLES

Explanation

Creating mind images is easier when readers know how to use the right text clues. While engaging them in an irresistible riddle game, this lesson helps students form visualizations and then home in on and pinpoint a specific image. A natural parallel writing lesson would highlight parts of speech so that students can understand better how authors create descriptions that in turn spur readers' images.

Skill Focus

Creating mental images when reading; using graphics as information sources; developing vocabulary from concrete experiences

Materials & Resources

Text

- Any grade-appropriate text (Used in this lesson: *Fire on the Mountain* by Jane Kurtz)

- Photocopies, 1 for each student, of different brief text selections

Other

- A transparency of 1 page from the selected text

Bonus Ideas

Here's a great way to raise students' awareness of "colorful" language. Give small groups each a pack of crayons and a sheet of paper. Assign each a different color range such as red/orange, blue/green, or brown/black. Each group is to create a color chart about their color range. Encourage them to use rich vocabulary for their descriptions—as a start, they can refer to the names on the side of the crayon wrappers! Display these charts in the writing center for students' ongoing reference.

STEPS

1. Review with students the importance of forming mind pictures as they read. Explain that some text points lend themselves to visualizing more than others. For example, when an author describes objects, people, animals, or other concrete things, it's especially important that readers pause to form mind pictures. Explain further that the nouns, pronouns, and adjectives are essential to almost all descriptions, so these parts of speech can offer particular clues. Tell students that you'll look for those words as you read aloud today.

2. Display the text page transparency. Tell students that you'll underline words that you might visualize easily. Read the text aloud and use a transparency pen to underline key nouns, pronouns, and adjectives. An example based on the sample text follows:

   He walked by waterfalls and watched baboons leap in the trees. He played his flute and dreamed his dreams. An ibis turned its black, black head to listen as Alemaya passed.

3. Tell students that you're thinking specifically of one image from this paragraph. Their job is to use a set of riddles you'll provide and to guess which particular item you're focusing on. Below is an example set of riddle clues, with possible student guesses shown in parentheses:

   It has two eyes. (Could be Alemaya, the ibis, or the baboon)
   It has hair. (Could be Alemaya or the baboon)
   It lives in the trees. (It's the baboon!)

   Follow the same procedure for this second riddle:
   It has limbs. (Could be the tree, Alemaya, or the baboon)
   But it cannot walk. (It's the tree!)

4. Now, invite students to try this same exercise. Distribute photocopies of different brief text selections or text excerpts. Instruct students to read their selections carefully and then to underline the concrete items—things that they can touch, hear, see, smell, or taste. Following your model, they should write a set of riddle questions to see if others can guess which item they're focusing on. Have students share their riddles with the whole class and/or with partners.

STOP, LOOK, AND TELL

Prior to the Lesson: Recruit a student who will be willing to model with you. Select a student who has good verbal skills and who understands the concept of visualizing. Review the entire lesson with the student, especially what his or her role is. Also, ahead of time, check through the selected text and identify logical intervals for pausing and picturing. Depending upon the length and nature of the text, this might be every sentence, every paragraph, every column, or every page.

STEPS

1. Remind students that good readers are always visualizing—or seeing movies in their minds—during reading. Today you're going to give students a strategy that will help them remember to visualize every time they read.

2. Invite your student helper to come forward. Display the selected text. Tell the class that as you read, both you and your partner are going to be paying extra special attention to pictures you're forming in your minds based on the text. Point out that you've used VIP strips ahead of time to mark logical spots in the text for pausing.

3. With your partner, begin to read the text aloud chorally (simultaneously in unison). Stop at the first place you've marked. Say something like, "Okay, this is the first spot where my partner and I are going to try really hard to see in our minds the pictures we're forming based on what we're reading." Be sure students realize that you're not going to retell what you've read. Instead, each of you will describe the setting, characters, or anything else that can be seen with the eyes.

4. After several moments, turn to your partner. Say, "Now let's tell each other what we've seen so far." One possible set of visualizations, based on the sample text, follows:

Text	What You Might Share
Most bears' eyes have round pupils. Pandas have eyes like cats. That is why the Chinese call the panda "giant bear cat." Pandas can see very well because of their cat-like eyes.	"I'm seeing a round, black and white face with oval-shaped eyes that have slits and are blinking like a cat's."
	What Your Partner Might Share
	"I have a cat and I keep seeing my cat's eyes on a big, cuddly panda face."

5. Now tell students it's their turn. Set up partner groups. Give each student a sticky note cut into VIP strips. Using either assigned or independent reading texts, students should look ahead through several pages of text and place their sticky strips on logical stopping spots. Then they should read either chorally with their partners or individually and follow the Stop, Look, and Tell procedure that you've modeled. Bring the class together afterward to discuss comparisons among the images partners formed.

Using an Artist's Storyboard

Explanation

As your students become better at visualizing text, they will enjoy trying to create a storyboard. This storyboard will help them both to visualize and to better grasp the literary elements contained in a narrative. In this lesson, you first model how to work with the storyboard and then you invite students to use their own artistic sensibilities and abilities.

Skill Focus

Creating mental images when reading; using graphics as information sources; identifying characters, setting, and plot in a literary work

Materials & Resources

Text

- A narrative text with story elements that are easy to visualize (Used in this lesson: *When Abraham Talked to the Trees* by Elizabeth Van Steenwyk)

-

Other

- Transparency of the Artist's Storyboard (Appendix, p. 123)

- Photocopies, 1 for each student, of the Artist's Storyboard

Bonus Ideas

Invite students to cut apart the sections of their completed Artist's Storyboard. Create a bulletin board with headings such as "How We Saw the Character." Post students' sections under each heading. This will serve to illustrate how all readers process text differently.

Steps

1. Review with students the importance of readers' visualizing scenes and characters as they read a story. Remind the class that an illustrator doesn't typically talk with an author to find out exactly what he or she intended to portray. Book illustrators base their drawings only on the movies they see in their minds as they read the author's words. Tell students you're going to read a story to them today and draw what you see just as if you were an illustrator.

2. Display the transparency. Read through what each of the boxes calls for: the main character, the setting, the problem, several plot events, the solution, and the conclusion. Explain that as you read today, you'll be thinking especially about those text elements and trying to gather clues to help you visualize them as clearly as possible.

3. Read aloud the text you've selected. Stop at appropriate spots (for example, at a description of the main character or just after the problem is presented) and think aloud about what you're visualizing. Then sketch in a corresponding simple illustration on the transparency. Point out that sometimes, just as good readers need to, you'll have to fill in gaps when clues aren't given.

4. For the character box for the sample text, your think-aloud and sketching might be as follows:

Text Read Aloud	Accompanying Think-Aloud	Corresponding Sketch (on Artist's Storyboard)
Abraham gathered his mixed-together family around him before he stepped on a stump in the clearing beside the cabin. Other folks came too. Then he repeated the sermons he'd heard, word for word. Again and again and again.	"I'm thinking that the young Abraham Lincoln was probably tall and very thin just as he was when he was president. I'm picturing him standing on a tree stump talking."	[Your sketch of: A tall, thin boy standing on a tree stump]

5. Distribute a photocopy of the Artist's Storyboard (Appendix, p. 123) to each student. Using either a new section of the sample text or a different assigned or independent text, invite students to follow the same process you have modeled. Be sure to remind students that the art is only a sketch—they do not need to spend time perfecting their drawings. You might also suggest that they add brief captions to their drawings.

CREATING A "HOLLYWOOD MOVIE" TO VISUALIZE CHARACTER, SETTING, AND ACTIONS

···○ Explanation

To get students to visualize a story, try giving them a whole different perspective. Most students have a bit of Hollywood movie savvy. This lesson will tap that interest while giving them a purpose for their reading. They'll need to look closely at the clues in the text and visualize what an author is really describing as they attempt to become top Hollywood directors!

···○ Skill Focus

Creating mental images when reading; using graphics as information sources and as a means of organizing information logically; identifying characters, setting, and plot in a literary work

···○ Materials & Resources

Text

- A narrative text with story elements that are easy to visualize (Used in this lesson: *Leah's Pony* by Elizabeth Friedrich)

Other

- Transparencies of Directors' Forms (Appendix, p. 124)

- Photocopies, the appropriate one for each student crew, of Directors' Forms

···○ Bonus Ideas

As different crews present their plans, you might create a matrix chart to display the unique features of each. Then, invite the class to discuss whether all the different interpretations of the different crews mesh well into one final film.

Prior to the Lesson: Make several copies of the selected text available to students for several days before this lesson. Recommend that they read it through and become familiar with it. Using the wordings provided at right as a model, write on oversized paper the descriptions of five different "Hollywood Movie Directors' Crews." Post these descriptions in your classroom, with space provided under each for student names. Tell students that in the near future they will be pretending to "film" the book they've read. They are to browse through the descriptions and to sign up for a specific crew. (Alert the class ahead of time that after everyone has signed up, you may have to make adjustments yourself to balance out the numbers of each crew.) Note that if you feel you'd rather work with only four crews, the final one listed (Stage Directors) is probably the best choice to eliminate as it's the most difficult for this age group.

Directors
Casting Directors—Your job is to decide how many roles will be cast for the movie and to write a clear description of what physical characteristics and personality traits the characters should have.
Scenery Directors—Your job is to decide how many different locations will be used for the filming and to provide details of what each should look like.
Costume Directors—Your job is to decide what each character should wear and to describe details of what each costume should look like.
Prop Directors—Your job is to decide what materials, objects, and equipment should be in the scenes and to provide necessary details about these items.
Stage Directors—Your job is to decide and describe (for at least one scene) the movements that the characters will need to make.

STEPS

1. On the day of the lesson, take down the directors' sheets and announce that today is the day students will all become Hollywood directors! Read aloud each description and the names of the members of each final student crew (be sure you've made your final adjustments for numbers and any other considerations ahead of making the announcement).

2. Read aloud the selected story, which should by now be familiar to students. Then model the kinds of decisions that the different student crews are expected to make. Point out explicitly that you are supporting each of your decisions with clues from the text. An example set of decisions (for the Casting Directors) based on the sample text follows:

   > We know that Leah will need to be cast for this movie. She's the main character. Here are the clues we found for what she should look like and how she should act. First, she is a female. We think she should be around 10 to 12 years old. She's old enough to care for a pony and to ride it alone and old enough to go to town by herself. On page 125, the author tells us that she brushes her horse and rubs him under his chin. So, we think she needs to be a caring, loving person.

3. Organize the class into the crews you have announced. Distribute a photocopy of the appropriate Directors' Forms to each crew. Provide time for each crew to fill out the form. After each team has had an opportunity to read and study the text and to fill out their forms, have the different crews inform the class of the decisions they've made. Be sure they include text details and can provide text-based reasons for their choices.

PICTURE THAT WORD

Prior to the Lesson: Locate three to five important words in the selected text; each should be critical to the meaning of the text and useful for students to know in their own reading and writing. Note that this lesson may be implemented in two different ways. You might use it a) before students have had any exposure to a particular text, or b) shortly after students have read a text. In the first case, it's best to choose words that are likely already in students' listening vocabulary. In the second case, it's best to choose key words that need to be reviewed. (The lesson below illustrates the second scenario.)

STEPS

1. Explain to students that making a personal connection with a word is a real aid in remembering the meaning of the word. One great way to make a connection is to draw a picture of what the word means: This can help readers much more than merely memorizing a definition. Tell students that in today's lesson the class will first play a kind of word guessing game for critical words in the text, and then, once the words have been identified, they will have a chance to illustrate them.

2. On the board or on a transparency, draw a line to represent each letter of the words you've selected. An example follows:

   1. __ __ __ __ __ __ __ (7)

   2. __ __ __ __ __ __ __ __ __ (9)

   3. __ __ __ __ __ (5)

3. Ask students to think back to the key words highlighted in their earlier reading of the text. Focus on the first word in the list. Provide a loose hint about the meaning and have students examine the number of letters in the word. Can they guess what the word is?

4. Invite students to say the word they have guessed, but do not confirm or deny it. Instead, ask them to give you the first letter of the word. Immediately afterward reveal the correct first letter. If the guessed letter and the one you revealed are the same, ask them to give you the next letter and then reveal yours, and so on for the word's subsequent letters.

5. If the letter they guess and the correct letter are not the same, respond, "Then, could it be the word you were thinking of?" Giving them time to consider this question will help them both analyze the word and focus on its spelling.

6. Continue questioning, revealing letters, and cross-checking for correctness until the whole word is revealed. At this point, talk about the meaning of the word and how it relates to the text. The first word in the example from Step 2 would now be revealed as:

   1. p y r a m i d (7)

7. Next, distribute a sheet of unlined paper to each student. Instruct students to hold the paper horizontally, fold it in half, and then in half again. Finally, they should fold it from top to bottom. When they unfold the sheet, the creases should create eight rectangular sections.

8. In one section, have students write the word you've just identified and discussed. Invite them to sketch something quickly that will help them remember what the word means. (If the word represents an abstract concept, demonstrate how you can nonetheless make concrete associations with the word that allow you to illustrate it. For example, for a word like *bravery*, you might make an association with *sword* or *medal*, which could be depicted easily.) The folded sheet, with a completed entry for the example word, might look like this:

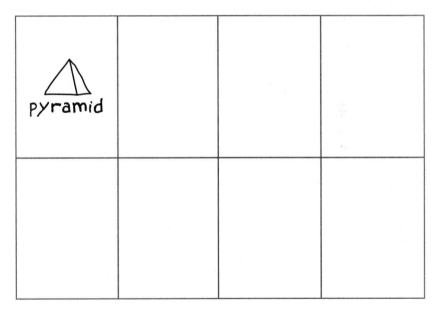

9. Continue with this process for the remaining words you've listed. At the conclusion of the lesson, students will have created a personal "glossary" of illustrations for critical words in the text selection. Sum up by reminding students of the essential element in this strategy: Once you've identified and explored a word, create a mental image of something that will help you remember the word's meaning. Picture it alongside the word and try to recall both the word and the image in the future.

READING THE PICTURES

Prior to the Lesson: *First, choose a text page on which graphics convey important information. Use sticky notes to cover all the words on your chosen page, leaving only the graphics (photographs, graphs, charts, illustrations) and any captions you feel might be critical for reasonable interpretation of the graphics. Make a transparency of this prepared page. Next, choose another text page on which the graphics also convey key information. Using sticky notes, prepare this page just as you did the first. Make photocopies (one for each partner pair or small group) of this page.*

STEPS

1. Tell students that this lesson will demonstrate how useful and efficient graphics and visuals can be for communicating information and ideas. You might share the old saying "A picture is worth a thousand words," and invite the class to offer their own opinions about why this might be true.

2. Display the prepared transparency. Explain that good readers pay careful attention to the graphics and visuals on every text page. In fact, they read the visuals just as they read the text because they know they might otherwise miss important information.

3. Model for students how you read and study the graphic(s) on the transparency. In the blank space where the text has been covered, write a summary of your interpretation of the graphic.

4. Now tell students it's their turn. Organize the class into partners or small groups. Distribute to each pair or group the photocopy of the similarly prepared page. Have students read the graphic(s), discuss what they think the graphic is saying, and write a brief summary in the blank space on the photocopied page.

5. When students have finished, bring the class back together to compare how different groups interpreted the graphic.

6. To close, display a transparency (or distribute photocopies) of the full page, with text and graphics. Have students discuss whether the information in the picture enhances the printed text or whether the visuals give new information. Encourage students to discuss, as well, whether the author and text publishers have made the best use of the graphic—does it relate well to the text, is it positioned appropriately, and is it a clear representation?

Explanation

Second- and third-grade students are able to grasp the deeper uses of graphics and visuals in text and to understand that they can be as important as print in communicating information and ideas. Students may not place the same value on them, however, unless we stress that pictures must be "read" just as text is. This lesson engages them in a fun activity that teaches them to scrutinize and learn from graphics when there is no text on a page to fall back on.

Skill Focus

Creating mental images when reading; using graphics such as charts, pictures, and graphic organizers as information sources and as a means of organizing information logically

Materials & Resources

Text

- An informational text, such as your science, social studies, or other content book, with graphics as well as text

Other

- Several sticky notes
- A transparency of a specially prepared page (see "Prior to the Lesson" notes)
- For each small group or partner pair, a photocopy of a similarly prepared page
- Photocopies or a transparency of the full, uncovered page students are working with

TWO-PART LESSON: FIGURES OF SPEECH AND POETIC DEVICES

PART 1: RECOGNIZING PICTURES AND SOUNDS IN TEXT

Explanation

The high-quality literature used in second and third grade can provide you with many opportunities to show students how skillful authors craft their language to help readers paint pictures and hear sounds in their minds. This lesson not only calls attention to the wonderful imagery and poetic devices good writers use, it also helps students realize that different senses are involved in a reader's perceiving and appreciating figurative language.

Skill Focus

Using graphics such as charts, pictures, and graphic organizers as information sources and as a means of organizing information logically; identifying figurative language and other poetic devices such as similes, metaphors, onomatopoeia, and alliteration to enhance understanding

Materials & Resources

Text

- Multiple copies of a grade-appropriate text that uses several different types of figures of speech and poetic devices—for example, similes, metaphors, onomatopoeia, or alliteration (Used in this lesson: *Moonflute* by Audrey Wood)

Other

- 1 or 2 sticky notes for each student

STEPS

1. Tell students that today's lesson is a search for the answer to this question: Why do authors choose the particular words that they use?

2. Display the selected text and read it aloud, just for students' enjoyment.

3. After the reading, discuss with the class why the text is moving and powerful. Guide the discussion to focus on the effectiveness of the text's rich figurative language. Say something like, "Now that we've enjoyed the whole book, I want us to pay attention to certain words that the author chose—words that help us really see and hear what we're reading!"

4. On one side of the board, draw a large ear. Leave a good deal of space around it. On the other side, draw a large eye with similar space around it.

5. Read aloud selected text passages that are particularly rich in poetic or evocative sounds. Below is an example from the sample book (with important sounds underlined):

   Ghostly white and gnarled tree trunks crowded close together. Fat vines hung from their limbs, looping like giant snakes from tree to tree.

   Follow your reading with a comment like this: "Close your eyes and let me read this again. Tell me what you hear in the mixture of sounds." Read the passage again, stressing especially any evocative sounds. In the sample passage, students should begin to hear something moving through the thick forest.

6. Near the ear you've drawn, write the lines from the text passage above.

7. Next, read aloud selected text passages that include figures of speech. Below is an example from the sample book:

   Soon Firen was not flying—she was speeding through the sky like a rocket firecracker . . . .

   Follow your reading with a comment like this: "The author says that Firen looks like a rocket firecracker. I've seen rocket firecrackers on the 4th of July, and that really gives me a picture in my mind of how Firen looks as she blazes across the sky! Often authors say something new or unusual looks like something familiar to help us get a good picture in our minds."

8. Set up small groups. Distribute a copy of the selected text and one or two sticky notes to each student. Have student groups look through the text for a word, a phrase, or a sentence that demonstrates particularly powerful words. The words they choose must help them see or hear especially well what they are reading. Have a volunteer from each group come forward to place their sticky notes appropriately on the board—either next to the ear or next to the eye.

TWO-PART LESSON: FIGURES OF SPEECH AND POETIC DEVICES

PART 2: CATEGORIZING PICTURES AND SOUNDS IN TEXT

Explanation

Once students understand the purposeful word choices that authors make, they are ready to look at expressive language in greater detail and to learn about the various categories of figures of speech and poetic devices. In this second part of the lesson, students work with the same text and, with your guidance, classify its figurative language according to standard terms and definitions.

Skill Focus

Using graphics such as charts, pictures, and graphic organizers as a means of organizing information logically; identifying figurative language and other poetic devices such as similes, metaphors and alliteration

Materials & Resources

Text

- The same text used in Part 1 (Used in this lesson: *Moonflute* by Audrey Wood)

Other

- Students' sticky notes from Part 1

- A transparency or the chalkboard

Bonus Ideas

Create "whisper phones" (tubes made of PVC pipe in the shape of phones) to allow students to explore text that has rich figurative and poetic language. With the tubes in hand, partners (or individuals) can read their favorite lines aloud softly and in their best voices, without disturbing others.

STEPS

1. Tell students that in this part of the lesson, they will learn the names for some of the devices and figures of speech they worked with in Part 1 of this lesson and they will get a chance to put the text words into appropriate categories.

2. On the board or a transparency, draw an ear as you did in Part 1. This time, extend the ear into a hierarchical chart that includes the correct terminology for poetic devices. Under each of the three key terms—onomatopoeia, alliteration, assonance/consonance—draw a large rectangular box. Write one example of each device within the appropriate box. (See Step 5.)

3. Follow the same procedure for the eye, using the key terms simile, metaphor, and personification. (See Step 5.)

4. Invite students to come forward to position their sticky notes from Part 1 within the appropriate category. A note of caution: Often figures of speech overlap and fit into more than one category correctly. For these young students, your main goal is to achieve overall awareness of the different kinds of language that writers use.

5. Below are two hierarchical charts based on the sample text, one for the ear (poetic devices) and one for the eye (figures of speech). The material in the boxes represents the examples from students' sticky notes.

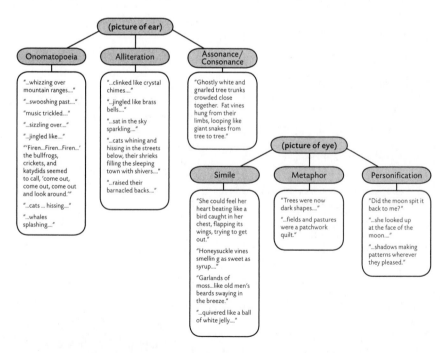

Accessing Prior Knowledge

Because prior knowledge plays a critical role in comprehension of text, as students grow and learn and widen their experience base, the potential for making meaning in their reading increases with every year. We can say this with certainty because we now know that reading is an active process of meaning construction in which readers connect old knowledge with new information they encounter in the text (Harris and Hodges, 1995). If we envision this process as a formula, it would be: Old knowledge plus new knowledge equals comprehension. Thinking about it this way helps to highlight two important factors involved in teaching young readers. First, students often assume they have a one-way relationship with the printed page: It's there to tell them everything. An important part of the teacher's job is to help students realize they bring a great deal to the page. Rather than one-way, the relationship is always interactive. Second, because every reader brings a different, indeed unique, constellation of experiences and knowledge to the page, every reader is reading and comprehending uniquely.

The lessons in this section are primarily intended to help you develop the first factor—students' ability to call upon and make use of the background knowledge that they already have. Before saying a bit more about that, it's important to point out that frequently a teacher must go beyond helping students retrieve knowledge and must, in addition, actually help them build that knowledge. Many children, especially low achievers, have had limited experiences in their young lives. They have significant gaps in their exposure to text and world knowledge.

Good teachers are aware of this with every lesson they teach, realizing that a key part of their work is to help such students lay that all-important foundation. If the class is studying Great Britain and some children have never left the boundaries of their community, a teacher needs to pull down the map, go to the Internet to do research, show them pictures, and engage them in discussions to give them experiences that will help to make them successful. Only when the reader can associate a text with memories and experiences does it become anchored in the reader's mind (Keene and Zimmermann, 1997). Staying mindful of this daily certainly takes effort on the teacher's part. But when comprehension is the reward, the payoff for both student and teacher is immense and worth all the effort.

You'll find that the lessons in this section use different ways to tap into (and sometimes to build upon) students' prior knowledge. In three lessons, you'll ask them to make different kinds of connections—text-to-self, text-to-text, and text-to-the-world—to get ready for reading with comprehension. In several other lessons, you'll help students identify and sort out their "knew" knowledge from their "new" learning. For example, they'll have a chance to use anticipation guides to declare before reading what they feel they know about a topic and then to discover afterward whether their prereading knowledge was accurate. And because

A teacher guides a student to make predictions based on the cover of a magazine.

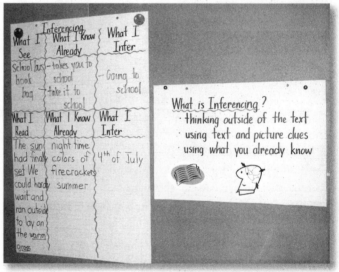

After presenting and discussing a chart that defines the skill of inferencing, this teacher uses another chart to record students' inferences from illustrations and from text.

inferring is at the very heart of meaning construction for learners of all ages (Anderson and Pearson, 1984), a lesson focused on making inferences is included. Here, you'll model for students how to link their own world knowledge with text clues to answer a key inferential question about a text.

Let's take a look now at different ways you can prepare students to approach the printed page. Your goal is clear: to give them a better sense of how what they already know can help them come away from the page knowing even more.

CONNECTING WITH WHAT YOU KNOW

Explanation

This is the first of a series of three lessons introducing the three basic kinds of connections that good readers make consistently before and during reading. Comprehension depends to a great degree upon connections readers make between their personal experiences and the text. Also known as text-to-self connections, this relationship is a critical one to call to students' attention.

Skill Focus

Making connections among texts read aloud or independently and prior knowledge, other texts, and the world; monitoring comprehension

Materials & Resources

Text

- Any grade-appropriate fiction or nonfiction text about which you can make personal connections (Used in this lesson: *Saturdays and Teacakes* by Lester Laminack)

- Multiple copies of a text about which students can make connections

Other

- 1 sticky note for each student

- Poster paper or butcher paper

- Markers

Bonus Ideas

Have students jot down personal connections they have made during independent reading. Invite them to choose one special one to illustrate. Gather the pictures and attach them to a roll of colored paper to create a text-to-self "quilt" to display on the classroom wall.

STEPS

1. Tell students that good readers make several kinds of connections before and during reading. Today's lesson will focus on "text-to-self " connections: These are the kind readers make between their own lives and the events in a book. Text-to-self connections involve using what you already know to help you understand new information better.

2. Mount the sheet of poster paper and title it "Text-to-Self Connections." Under the title, write a brief definition based on your explanation in Step 1. Leave a good deal of free space on the poster.

3. Read to or with your students a story about which you can make some easy personal connections. For example, for the sample text, you might pause after encountering a section of text that jogs your memory and share, "What's described here reminds me so much of when my grandmother used to make biscuits for me. She would get me to stick my finger in the freshly baked dough and then she would fill the hole I made with syrup. Yummmm! I can still remember how warm, buttery, and sweet those biscuits were. I don't think I've ever had one as good since those days. Because I was able to make this connection, the story really came alive for me. This boy rides his bike to his grandmother's house just the way I used to do, too! I loved the freedom of going to her house alone."

4. Now tell students it's their turn. Distribute the book you've selected for students. Instruct them to read it through once.

5. Give a sticky note to each student. Have them find at least one thing in the text that reminds them of something in their own lives. Once they've identified something, they should write it on the sticky note.

6. Invite students to come forward and to attach their sticky notes to the poster you've made. Have each student briefly describe the connection they've made and tell how it helped them understand the text better.

CONNECTING WITH OTHER TEXTS

Explanation

This second lesson in a series of three introduces text-to-text connections. This type builds as the literary history of a reader grows: As readers encounter new texts, they construct increasingly deeper understanding by drawing on what they have learned from prior texts. Students need to know just how powerful their own literary history is. They need to read, read, read!

Skill Focus

Making connections among texts read aloud or independently and prior knowledge, other texts, and the world; monitoring comprehension

Materials & Resources

Text

- Any grade-appropriate fiction or nonfiction text about which you can easily make a connection with something else you've read (Used in this lesson: *The Wednesday Surprise* by Eve Bunting and *Mr. Henry Baker* by Amy Hest)

Other

- Banner saying "Books Connect with Other Texts"

- Bulletin board

- Multiple photocopies of book cover outlines

- Markers or crayons

- Stapler

Prior to the Lesson: Prepare bulletin board space for use in this lesson and in the future. Make a banner that says "Books Connect with Other Texts," and place it in the center of the display space. On two photocopied book cover outlines (see diagram at right), write the titles of the two sample books. Color the covers if you'd like (or have a student do that for you). Alternately, you might copy the covers onto pastel paper. Staple the covers about 12 inches apart on your bulletin board display. On a cabinet nearby, place additional copies of the book cover outline.

STEPS

1. Review with students what they learned in the previous lesson—that good readers use personal experiences to make connections with texts. Explain that that's only one kind of possible connection. Sometimes readers may not personally have had an experience that helps them understand the text. Then they can think about other books or texts they've read that help them make a connection.

2. Read aloud a selection that will be easy to connect with another text that has been previously read in the class. For example, if the class has already read the first sample text, *The Wednesday Surprise*, you might now read the second, *Mr. Henry Baker*. Model your thinking as shown below:

   > This really reminds me of a book that we read about a grandmother who learned to read. Do you recall that story? In this story, the man is 100 years old and is learning to read for the first time! That's amazing, isn't it? In *The Wednesday Surprise*, the grandmother was learning to read for the first time, too. Isn't it wonderful that older adults still want very much to learn to read? I'm thinking that these books were different in some ways. In *Mr. Henry Baker*, the man learned to read at school. He went every day with his first-grade friend who was also learning to read. In *The Wednesday Surprise*, the granddaughter was the one teaching her grandmother to read. But both stories had young children helping other people in some way. It's really good to compare similar books in your mind. Often I find that it helps me to understand what I'm reading better if I can relate it to something else I've read. This is called a text-to-text connection.

3. Call attention to the bulletin board display. Tell students that this display is for current and future use. Point out the two decorated book covers, mounted on the bulletin board. Draw a line between them. Write along the line the major connection you've made between the two books. For example, for the two sample books, you might write, "The older adults in these books are both learning to read and have young people to help them."

4. Tell students that for future assigned and independent reading books, they should feel free to add to the display. When they have made a connection between two books, they should follow your model: Using two book cover outlines from the stack, they should title and decorate the covers, mount them, and explain the connection.

CONNECTING TEXT TO THE WORLD AROUND US

Explanation

This final lesson in a series of three focuses on text-to-world connections. Readers bring not only their own personal and literary histories to their reading, they also bring their world knowledge. The more they know about historical and current events and happenings in science, the greater their world knowledge. Even students at these young ages have learned things about the world at large that they need to be able to tap into. This lesson will help them do just that.

Skill Focus

Making connections among texts read aloud or independently and prior knowledge, other texts, and the world; monitoring comprehension

Materials & Resources

Text

- Any grade-appropriate fiction or nonfiction text about which you can easily make a connection with your world knowledge (Used in this lesson: *Mama: A True Story in Which a Baby Hippo Loses His Mama During a Tsunami but Finds a New Home, and a New Mama* by Jeanette Winter)

Other

- Banner saying, "Books Connect to the World"

- Bulletin board

- Picture (perhaps downloaded from the Internet) of a world map or globe

- Multiple photocopies of book cover outlines (see p. 82)

- Markers or crayons

- Stapler

Prior to the Lesson: Expand the bulletin board space you created in the previous lesson. Make a banner that says "Books Connect to the World," and place it in the center of the display space. Next to or just under the banner, attach a picture of a world map or globe. On a photocopied book cover outline (see page 82), write the title of the sample book. Color the cover if you'd like (or have a student do that for you). Alternately, you might copy the cover onto pastel paper. Staple the cover about 12 inches away from the map or globe on your bulletin board display. On a cabinet nearby, place additional copies of the book cover outline (or add to the stack you started in the previous lesson).

STEPS

1. Briefly review with students what they learned in the previous two lessons. Explain that there is a third kind of connection readers need to make. Sometimes readers need to think beyond their own personal lives and reading experiences to their knowledge of the larger world to better understand a text. We refer to this as making "text-to-world" connections.

2. Read aloud a selection that will be easy to connect with a familiar world event. For example, the sample text is the story of an animal that lost its mother in the 2004 tsunami that struck Indonesia and Southeast Asia. After reading you might model your thinking as shown below:

   > Boys and girls, this text really makes me think about something I've read a lot about in the newspapers and heard a lot on the news—a terrible hurricane called Katrina that happened in New Orleans in 2005. People and animals died in that storm, too, and many homes were destroyed. Some children wound up living in other cities and had to be reunited with their parents later. Because I know so much about that terrible storm, it helped me understand this story better, which tells about a hippo that lost its mother in the great Indonesian tsunami of 2004. Connecting all those things I know about Katrina to this little hippo helps me really feel and picture this story better.

3. Call attention to the bulletin board display and the additional banner. Explain to students that you've now expanded the display from the previous lesson. Point out the decorated book cover and the world map or globe you've mounted on the bulletin board. Draw a line between them. Write along the line the major connection you've made between the world and the book. For example, for the sample book, you might write, "This book tells of a terrible storm like the storm called Katrina that I know about from the news."

4. Tell students that in the future, for both assigned and independent reading books, they should feel free to add to the display. When they feel they have made a connection between their world knowledge and a book they've read, they should follow your model: They should title and decorate a book cover outline from the stack, mount it on the bulletin board, attach it to the map or globe, and explain the connection.

Knew/New Charts

◇························◇

Explanation

Frequently, young students don't realize how much they've learned during their school day or during their reading of a particular text. Sorting out prior knowledge from what is unfamiliar in a text can help them better appreciate both the "knew" and the "new." This lesson provides an opportunity for students to use a simple chart to do just that.

Skill Focus

Making connections among texts read aloud or independently and prior knowledge, other texts, and the world; monitoring comprehension

Materials & Resources

Text

- Any text about which you can easily distinguish old knowledge from new information (Used in this lesson: *Pirates* by Will Osborne and Mary Pope Osborne)

- Multiple copies of a similar text or selection for student use

Other

- Transparency or the chalkboard

- 1 sheet of paper for each set of partners or individual

Bonus Ideas

Write *Know* and *No* on separate sheets of paper. Have one student create a statement based on information from a text and read it aloud. He or she then calls on a student who needs to point to *Know* if this statement is true (based on what was learned) or *No* if they think it is false. See if students can stump each other.

Steps

1. Explore the words *knew* and *new* with your students—words that sound alike but are spelled in different ways. On a transparency or the board, write the two words side by side. Draw a line dividing them into two columns to create a simple T-chart. Add a few basic graphics next to the words to help students distinguish between the two. (For example, for *knew* you might draw a profile of a head with the outline of a brain inside. For *new*, you might sketch a few rays emanating from the word itself to indicate something that's shiny and fresh.)

2. Tell students that these two words are important to good readers. Good readers realize that what they *knew* about a topic before starting to read will help them make better sense of the *new* information they meet in text.

3. Explain to students that when you reach for a book and read the title you immediately begin to think of what you already know about this topic. Model how you do just that—reach for a book or turn to a chapter and begin to brainstorm a "Knew" list of things you already know about the topic. For example, for the sample text, you might jot down a list like this:

   Knew

   - Pirates robbed people at sea.

   - Most stories of famous pirates relate things that happened long ago.

   - Pirates usually traveled in groups.

   - They terrorized people.

   Sum up by saying something like, "Boys and girls, look at all the things I know about pirates. I can really use this old knowledge to help me with what's new to me in this book. I'm going to read with that in mind."

4. Read aloud the preselected text. As you read, occasionally model how you encounter something familiar that the text has reminded you about. Add this information to the "Knew" list.

5. Think aloud, too, about any new information you discover as you read. Comment on those new facts or observations and add them to the "New" column in the chart. Most likely this column will not exceed the "Knew" list, but even if you add only one new item, this will illustrate that you've grown as a reader.

6. Finally, present students with a different topic and reading selection. Distribute sheets of paper to individuals or partners. Have them create their own "Knew/New" charts to keep track of what they knew versus what they've learned. Ask them to share their results with the class.

ANTICIPATION GUIDES

Explanation

Anticipation guides are a good example of the old saying "Everything old is new again." They were popular long ago, lost favor for a while, and recently have seen a (justified) revival. They so clearly and easily help students set their own goals for reading. What reader doesn't want to know that his or her guess was the right one?

Skill Focus

Making connections among texts read aloud or independently and prior knowledge, other texts, and the world; monitoring comprehension

Materials & Resources

Text

- Any grade-appropriate nonfiction text (Used in this lesson: *Nature's Amazing Partners* by Katharine Kenah)

Other

- 1 photocopy of an Anticipation Guide for each student (see "Prior to the Lesson")

- 1 sheet of paper for each student

Prior to the Lesson: *Read through your selected the material and jot down ten statements of fact. Change something in about half the statements so those statements are no longer true. Type your statements, print them out, and make one photocopy for each student.*

STEPS

1. Remind students that all readers bring a great deal of knowledge to each reading selection. This knowledge really helps readers understand what the selection means. Today they'll get to show what they already know or at least make a guess about what they think they might know. They may be surprised to find that they know more than they think they do!

2. Distribute the list of statements to students. An example Anticipation Guide, based on the sample text, is below:

Before		Nature's Amazing Partners	After		Page
T	F	Clown fish keep the sea anemones clean.	T	F	
T	F	The rhinoceros keeps the tickbird free of bugs.	T	F	
T	F	Sharks are "taxis" for remoras.	T	F	
T	F	Crocodiles let plovers (birds) clean their teeth.	T	F	
T	F	Starfish house small animals that the coral eats.	T	F	
T	F	The sea anemone hides hermit crabs.	T	F	
T	F	Elephants help egrets find food.	T	F	

3. Instruct students to circle or write whether they think each statement is true or false. Tell them it's all right to guess if they don't know, but they must respond to each statement. (Reassure students that an incorrect guess can be fixed during or after reading and that it's fine, even expected, to make mistakes during a pre-reading activity.) To better observe whether all students have responded to all points, you might have them give a thumbs up (true) or thumbs down (false) after they've made their guesses.

4. Read aloud the preselected text once through for enjoyment. Read it a second time, announcing each page number, so that students can check their responses carefully and revise any incorrect guesses. Ask them to jot down the page number on which the correct information is given.

5. Allow students to share and discuss the correct answers at the conclusion of the lesson. Stress that correctness is less important here than recognizing that all readers bring prior knowledge to the page as they read.

THE KNOWLEDGE CHAIN

Explanation

In this lesson, students have a chance to literally hold in their hands the building blocks of reading comprehension. As they make two different chains of "knew" and "new" understandings, abstract aspects of the reading process are made visible and students can celebrate their own learning.

Skill Focus

Making connections among texts read aloud or independently and prior knowledge, other texts, and the world; monitoring comprehension

Materials & Resources

Text

- Multiple copies of a grade-appropriate fiction or nonfiction text on a particular topic

Other

- Numerous 1 ½" strips of paper (white and pastel), cut into horizontal rows from standard sheets
- Tape or stapler
- Wire clothes hanger or large silver clasp (optional)

Bonus Ideas

Paper chains are a great way to build community spirit in the classroom, and they can even be used as incentives. For example, any time a student has a thoughtful question, a group performs well, or a student helps someone, a loop can be added to a growing classroom chain. Once the chain touches the floor, the class gets to celebrate—perhaps receiving an extra recess, free homework passes, a lesson held outside on a nice day, and so on.

STEPS

1. Review with students how important it is for readers to tap prior knowledge before reading about a topic. If a reader were to encounter only unfamiliar information in a text selection, he or she wouldn't achieve the same understanding possible for someone with prior knowledge of the topic.

2. Set up partners. Distribute two or more white paper strips to each pair. Invite students to brainstorm what they already know about a particular topic. Instruct them to write this information on the paper strips. They can use both sides of the strips if they wish.

3. Have all students connect their links into a chain. Help students secure the final link onto a wire clothes hanger or with a clasp.

4. Distribute the text selection to partners. Provide each partner set with two or more pastel paper strips. Instruct students to read the selection and to note new information on the paper strips. Students may note brand-new information that they discovered during the reading; they may also note corrected understandings (that is, revisions of their prior knowledge based on what they've just read). Again, they may write on both sides of the strips if they wish.

5. Now invite partners to link their strips together with those of other partner groups. The resulting long chain can be added to the links of prior knowledge, or displayed side by side with that chain. You might staple both chains (either singly or together) to the classroom bulletin board for all to examine.

6. Conclude by pointing out and discussing the two prongs of comprehension students have observed. While the class has grown in knowledge (look at all those pastel strips!), just as important is the knowledge that students began with (all those white strips). Without the prior knowledge, their learning would not have been as deep.

MAKING INFERENCES

STEPS

1. Review with students that authors don't tell their readers *everything*. Sometimes readers have to use text clues and think hard in order to figure out the meaning that lies beyond the words in a text. Today you'll model for students how readers gather clues in text, add that information to their own experiences, and construct meaning that isn't expressed directly in the text. This process is called *inferring* or *making inferences*.

2. Read aloud the preselected text. After reading, tell students you are left with a big question about the book. The book never answers that question directly. Write the question on the board or on a transparency. For the sample book, you might write:

   Why is Mr. George Baker learning to read?

3. Now tell students that even though the book didn't state why Mr. Baker was learning to read, you can *infer* the answer. Under your question, draw three columns.

4. Title the first column as shown below and then look back through the book to hunt for clues that might help you answer the question. Here is how the first column based on the sample book might look:

   The story said . . .
   - He's 100 years old.
   - He's going to school.
   - He's a famous musician.
   - He said (about not being able to read): "That must be corrected."

5. Title the second column as shown below and think aloud about things you know from your life's experiences that might answer the question. Try to relate some of these observations to the facts you've listed. Here is how the second column based on the sample book might look:

   . . . and I know this . . .
   - People don't usually have to go to school as adults.
   - No one would expect someone to go to school at 100.
   - Today we need to be able to read to make a living.
   - People who can't read often feel left out of our society.

6. Finally, title the third column, and write your inference within that column. Here is what the final column might look like for the sample book:

   . . . so I think this answers the question.
   He wants to read to make his life feel complete.

7. Point out that the three headings for these columns, when put together, can be read as a complete sentence. They combine to explain the process of making an inference.

Explanation

When readers infer, they use their prior knowledge and textual clues to draw conclusions and form unique interpretations of text (Miller, 2002). This lesson uses an evolving chart to demonstrate how readers put these two key ingredients together to form a meaningful inference.

Skill Focus

Making connections among texts read aloud or independently and prior knowledge, other texts, and the world; monitoring comprehension

Materials & Resources

Text
- Any text that implies but does not state directly an important message (Used in this lesson: *Mr. George Baker* by Amy Hest)

Other
- Transparency or chalkboard

Bonus Ideas

Here's an easy literacy center activity. Assemble simple pictures from newspapers or magazines along with a chart that has three headings like those in this lesson: (1) "The picture shows this…"; (2) "… and I know this . . ."; and (3) "… so I think this is what's happening." Students are to look at the pictures and fill in the chart with an inference about what they see. An example might be a picture of a man opening an umbrella. The chart would be filled out: (1) "A man is opening an umbrella." (2) "I know we use umbrellas when it's raining." (3) "I think he must be going outside where it's raining."

Summarizing

Summarizing is a far more sophisticated task than it first might appear to experienced readers. All too often, summarizing is confused with merely choosing what is most important in text, but genuine summarizing goes far beyond that simple activity (Dole, Duffy, Roehler, and Pearson, 1991). The summarizing process actually calls on a number of higher-level thinking skills. To be able to create a summary, you must be able to identify the main idea, leave out details sometimes including those connected to the main idea, generalize from text information, integrate ideas, and remove redundancy (NRPR; NICHHD, 2000). The reader must not only separate what is most important from what is of lesser importance, but he or she must also synthesize the prioritized information to form a new text, of sorts, that stands for the original text. A pretty tall order for a second or third grader!

However, if we do it appropriately by setting a foundation and then slowly introducing the concept, teaching our youngest readers about summarizing is not only possible—it's definitely worth the effort.

In fact, for a number of reasons, summarizing improves overall comprehension of text (Pearson and Duke, 2002). For example, summarizing can improve memory for what is read, both in terms of free recall and for answering questions (NRPR; NICHHD, 2000).

With the distinct benefits of teaching children to summarize in mind, we must also understand what research says is necessary for this learning to take place. Many, if not most, children require direct instruction in the different skills and subtasks involved in summarizing. The teacher's role is critical in explaining what must occur and in modeling how the process looks and sounds. Further, to produce good oral and written summaries of text, students must have adequate time for applying what they've learned and for practicing summarizing. With instruction and practice, not only will they become better at summarizing, they'll become better readers (Pearson and Duke, 2002).

As you'll see from the range of lessons in this section, summarization can take many forms, but the common thread is teaching students to see the big picture by looking for key pieces. In the first set of lessons, students learn to highlight what's important (main ideas, themes, and events), then to sort out significant supporting information, and, finally, to rejoin the pieces to create a successful summary. In later lessons, students identify key words and phrases as a preparatory step for summarizing. They also learn to neatly chunk narrative text into beginning, middle, and end and into core story elements like character, setting, and plot to create summaries. They employ captions and graphics as summarizing tools, fitting together the puzzle pieces to tell a story. Finally, they learn to internalize the main point of a story by looking at it through the story's "eyes" and their own eyes.

This girl stops to summarize what she has read and to share it with the class.

Capturing the essence of a reading selection is what summarizing is all about. It's a challenge that is far more sophisticated than it appears but the resulting enhanced comprehension is well worth the effort.

THREE-PART LESSON: IDENTIFYING WHAT'S WHAT TO WRITE A SUMMARY

PART 1: DETERMINING WHAT'S MOST IMPORTANT

···○ Explanation

This three-part lesson series gives students practice in a set of skills that they'll need at all grade levels, and even in college. In this first lesson, they'll learn to identify what's most important in a text and highlight it—the initial step in a methodical process that will lead to their creating a successful summary.

···○ Skill Focus

Summarizing main ideas, events, and themes in texts; recalling significant details in texts; categorizing and classifying ideas

···○ Materials & Resources

Text

- A brief, grade-appropriate informational text (Used in this lesson: original article based on information on aardvarks from www.enchantedlearning.com)

- A consumable, grade-appropriate magazine or newspaper for each partner set

Other

- A transparency of the selected text

- 2 highlighters in different colors for each partner set

- 1 sheet of chart paper

STEPS

1. Discuss with the class the basic elements of a summary. Define a summary as "a short way of telling the most important points in a text." A good summary includes the main idea and supporting details. Tell students that in this set of three lessons they will have the opportunity to summarize material from a detailed, descriptive essay. Their job in this first lesson will be to highlight what is most important—the main idea—in a text. You might let them know that the skill they learn today they will need even in college. (That should impress them!)

2. Mount a piece of blank chart paper. List guidelines for the process good readers follow to highlight a text's key ideas. Be sure to encourage students' participation and discussion as you create the chart. (This chart can be displayed permanently in your classroom for students' ongoing reference.) An example follows:

Guidelines for Highlighting the Most Important Ideas

1. Read the beginning and ending and look for an idea that is stated and later restated.

2. Look for key words that are often repeated.

3. Check to see if the big ideas are supported by interesting details, but don't confuse those interesting details with what's most important!

4. Never highlight more than half of the text.

5. Never highlight whole sentences—just words and phrases.

---

3. Display the transparency of the preselected text passage. Read the whole passage aloud one time, and then return to the beginning. Read each sentence and model how you decide whether that statement is important enough to highlight. Think aloud as you make your decisions. The sample text, with highlighting and think-aloud comments, is shown below.

Survival of the Earth Pig

Surprisingly little is known about aardvarks. Their name means "Earth pig" in the South African language. These mammals have a snout like a pig's, although much longer and narrower than a pig's snout. Most unique is the fact that the aardvark is an insectivore with many adaptations that make it successful at getting its food and nutrition. They hunt for their food at night and sleep during the day. Their long snout and big ears signal highly developed senses of smell and hearing that help them locate the ants and termites that make up their diet. When they find the meal, they use their large, hoof-like claws to dig into hills and mounds. An extremely long tongue and very sticky saliva help them get the insects out of their hiding places. They have only ten teeth in their cheeks and require no incisors or canines to chew the insects they eat. They are strange-looking critters by most standards, but their adaptations allow them to hunt and survive successfully!

"I'm assuming they're going to tell us something about the aardvark that is noteworthy—not just that little is known."

"This just seems to be a general description and not an important idea."

"Now the article is saying that there's something very special about the aardvark. I'll bet this is important. I'm going to highlight this part."

"Hmm, this piece is full of details about how the animal eats. It's really interesting, but I don't think this information is the main reason the author wrote this piece."

"It's still giving details about how it gets food."

"This last idea sounds very much like the part I highlighted. It seems to be making the same points again. So, I think I've highlighted the right part."

4. Set up partners. Distribute a magazine or newspaper and two different-colored highlighters to each pair. Have students select an article and use one highlighter as they go through the text the first time. Then, have them indicate final decisions (focusing on highlighting the fewest words possible) with the other color. (Be sure to retain students' articles to use in Part 2.)

Three-Part Lesson: Identifying What's What to Write a Summary

Part 2: Finding What Supports the Main Idea

Explanation

This lesson, the second in a three-part series, helps students prioritize text information as they prepare to write a summary. They have already identified the main idea in a piece. Now they search for the supporting details, which are often more intriguing than the key point. Therefore, this lesson also encourages students to differentiate between what is merely interesting and what is centrally important in text.

Skill Focus

Summarizing main ideas, events, and themes in texts; recalling significant details in texts; categorizing and classifying ideas

Materials & Resources

Text

- The text used in Part 1 of this lesson

- Partners' highlighted articles from Part 1

Other

- The highlighted text transparency from Part 1

- Blank transparency or chart paper

Steps

1. Tell students that today they will continue looking at the same text but this time they will focus on ideas that are less significant than those highlighted in Part 1. Only after they are able to identify both the key point(s) and the supporting details in a text will they be ready to summarize it. Warn students that these kinds of facts are sometimes so fascinating that they distract readers. Many readers remember these interesting tidbits and ignore the big picture or the main idea. Good readers always identify both the main idea and the details and always know the difference.

2. Display the text transparency. Read back through the article and underline the parts that offer details about the main idea you've already identified. A example of the sample text, with appropriate details underlined, follows:

Survival of the Earth Pig

Surprisingly little is known about aardvarks. Their name means "Earth pig" in the South African language. These mammals have a snout like a pig, although much longer and narrower than a pig's snout. Most unique is the fact that the aardvark is an insectivore with many adaptations that make it successful at getting its food and nutrition. They hunt for their food at night and sleep during the day. Their long snout and big ears signal highly developed senses of smell and hearing that help them locate the ants and termites that make up their diet. When they find the meal, they use their large, hoof-like claws to dig into hills and mounds. An extremely long tongue and very sticky saliva help them get the insects out of their hiding places. They have only ten teeth in their cheeks and require no incisors or canines to chew the insects they eat. They are strange looking critters by most standards but their adaptations allow them to hunt and survive successfully!

---

3. Next, using a new transparency or chart paper, create a simple T-chart to compare your findings and to illustrate the difference between what is simply interesting and what is important in a text selection. As you record supporting information, make the point that these interesting details all seem to support the main idea. They all tell why the aardvark's body and habits make it successful at getting food and surviving. Observe, "Boys and girls, we need to be able to separate what's important from what's interesting but not important in what we read. We need to be sure to see the main idea and not be distracted by what's simply interesting." The example on page 93 is based on the sample text.

What's Interesting (supporting details)	What's Important (main idea)
Highly developed smell and hearing	The aardvark has many adaptations that make it successful at getting food and nutrition for its survival.
Hoof-like claws	
Extremely long tongue	
Very sticky saliva	
Ten teeth in cheeks—no incisors or canines	

4. Set up the same partners who worked together on Part 1. Hand back their highlighted magazine or newspaper articles and have them follow your model to underline supporting details.

Three-Part Lesson: Identifying What's What to Write a Summary

Part 3: Writing the Summary

Explanation

This final lesson in the series demonstrates how all the pieces come back together in a concise, compact summary. You'll demonstrate how a reader can take what's most important, blend it with what's simply interesting, and rejoin these pieces to form a new whole—a summary that's nice and neat and that captures what the reader needs to remember!

Skill Focus

Summarizing main ideas, events, and themes in texts; recalling significant details in texts; categorizing and classifying ideas; responding to text through a variety of methods

Materials & Resources

Text

- The text used in Parts 1 and 2 of this lesson

- Partners' highlighted, underlined articles from Parts 1 and 2

Other

- Transparency of the highlighted, underlined text from Parts 1 and 2

- Transparency or chart paper draft of the T-chart from Part 2

Bonus Ideas

Try this approach when using content books. Have students draw a T-chart and list important points and supporting details. Then have them summarize the material.

Steps

1. Explain that once readers have figured out the main idea and supporting details of a text, they are ready to summarize it. Review with students that writing a summary is an effective way for readers to retain and recall what they have read.

2. Display both the transparency of the highlighted, underlined text and the T-chart. Tell students that the information you've already identified in this article is all you need to write a successful summary. Because you have determined both the main idea and the supporting details, you have already identified the essential information in the article. Now all you need to do is pull it back together.

3. Using the text transparency or the chalkboard, demonstrate for students how you write a summary based on your identified information. Model how you write the main idea (the first sentence) and follow that with the supporting details. Point out how you purposely condense the material and how you present it as briefly and concisely as possible. A summary is not the time for creative flourishes or elaboration! An example summary for the sample text follows:

   The aardvark's adaptations make it successful at getting its food for survival. It has a keen sense of smell and hearing to locate food and sharp, hoof-like claws for digging. It also has a long tongue, sticky saliva, and ten cheek teeth to get the food and chew it.

4. Re-form partner groups that worked together on Parts 1 and 2. Hand back their highlighted, underlined magazine or newspaper articles and have them follow your model to write summaries based on the information they have identified. When all have finished, invite partners to share their summaries with the whole class.

IDENTIFYING KEY WORDS AND PHRASES

Explanation

Identifying essential words and phrases in text is a fundamental part of both listening and reading comprehension. Once students know how to do this, they can far more effectively make written or mental notes and home in on what they need to remember. This lesson methodically walks students through this process and leaves them with two critical guidelines they can use on an ongoing basis.

Skill Focus

Summarizing main ideas, events, and themes in texts; recalling significant details in texts; categorizing and classifying ideas; using content/specialized words

Materials & Resources

Text

- A brief, grade-appropriate informational text with headings (Used in this lesson: First 2 pages of "Hail" in *Twisters and Other Terrible Storms* by Will Osborne and Mary Pope Osborne)

Other

- 10 standard index cards
- 1 pastel-colored index card
- Chart paper or chalkboard
- Pocket chart

Bonus Ideas

Organize students into groups. Provide all groups with index cards and the same textbook chapter. Have them record key words and phrases on the cards. Afterward, bring the class together to share and compare results and to discuss any differences.

Prior to the Lesson: *Read through your selected text to identify the key words and phrases. Identify as well interesting details that you will ultimately weed out during the process.*

STEPS

1. Explain to students that both readers and listeners need to know how to identify the really important points in text. This is an essential skill for comprehension. When good readers take notes, they focus on only the key points. They know that otherwise, they might wind up copying everything and that wouldn't help their understanding at all. And good listeners know that focusing on what's really important will help them respond to questions. Determining the key words and phrases in text is one really effective way for readers and listeners to focus on the important points. Today's lesson will help students learn to do just this: You'll read a section of text and show them how to determine the key words and phrases.

2. Display the preselected text and read aloud the chapter subheading, "Hail." Write this heading on a colored index card and place it at the top of the pocket chart. Point out that all the text's key words will relate to this topic. Say something like, "I'll be looking for key words that tell me more about this topic. *My key words will always connect directly to the topic or heading.*" Write this final statement on the board or chart paper so that students can use it as a guideline for their own work.

3. Read the text aloud. Think aloud as you show students how you decide whether to include a particular word or phrase. Explain that because this is an evolving process, some of the words and phrases you initially select may not prove to be essential. Write each word or phrase on a separate index card and place it randomly in the pocket chart. Below is a possible list of words and phrases and think-aloud commentary for the sample text:

   - **Hailstones or ice chunks**—"This part tells me that *hailstones* is another word used for *hail*. It helps me understand, too, that hail is the same as ice chunks. I bet the author will tell more about how these ice chunks are made. I'm thinking, too, that this is a kind of storm based on the title of this book, *Twisters and Other Terrible Storms.*"

   - **Forms when**—"I'll pay close attention to key words in this part since I want to know how hail is made."

   - **Cloud**—"The process of making hail seems to start in a cloud."

   - **Water droplet**—"It seems to start as a water droplet inside a tall cloud."

   - **Freezes**—"I'll make note that the water droplet freezes. That's certainly related to the ice chunks."

   - **Updraft**—"This is an important word because it is a burst of wind that causes the frozen droplet to fall back through the damp cloud."

   - **New layers**—"This explains that the droplet can get bigger and bigger and add more layers of ice every time it gets caught in the updraft and goes through a damp cloud again."

- **Heavy and falls**—"I see the word *finally* used right before this phrase. That's probably a signal that this is the last step in the process of forming a hailstone—the droplet has gotten too heavy to be lifted again, and it falls."

- **Rings inside**—"Here's an interesting fact. If you cut open a hailstone, you can see rings."

- **Times up and down**—"This is interesting, too. The rings show how many times a hailstone has been up and down through a cloud."

4. When all the index cards have been placed in the pocket chart, demonstrate how you determine the relative importance of each word or phrase. Think aloud as you move the cards about, ultimately placing the most important words/phrases at the top and the least essential at the bottom. Here's how the cards for the sample text might be arranged, along with an accompanying think-aloud commentary:

"Because the whole section is about hail or hailstones, I'll put this card toward the top. It restates the topic and gives a simple definition."

"The information on these two pages is really all about the whole process of how hail is formed. So this phrase is very important."

"These key words all describe the process of how hail is made. They will easily help me recall that process."

"This is a very interesting detail, but it's probably not something I would use to summarize what this section is about."

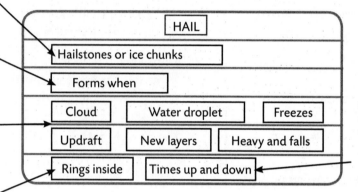

"Here's another smaller detail. It doesn't seem that important. I probably wouldn't need it in a summary."

5. Now show students how you reexamine and further analyze your selected words and phrases to make sure that you have targeted only those that are truly essential. Start by reminding students of the definition of a summary: "a short way of telling the most important points in a text." Then say something like, "Boys and girls, the two cards at the bottom of the chart give little details that are examples. They are not main ideas. To decide if I should remove them from the chart of truly key words, I ask myself, 'Can I summarize this chapter without those words?' I think I can. Here's my summary: *Hailstones are ice chunks that are formed from water droplets in clouds. The droplets freeze and are then sent back through damp clouds by updrafts until they are too heavy. Then they fall to the ground.* I think that tells exactly what this section is mainly about." Conclude by removing the two bottom cards from the chart.

6. Elicit students' help in adding a new guideline to the one you recorded on the board or chart paper in Step 2. Guide the class to generate a statement like the following: *Include only words that are required to summarize the text.*

SUMMARIZING A NARRATIVE: BEGINNING, MIDDLE, AND END

Explanation

In order to effectively summarize a piece of fiction, it's important to analyze its basic construction—beginning, middle, and end. It's also necessary to examine its core elements—character, setting, plot, problem, and solution. Here students use a graphic organizer to help them figure out structure and elements and to weave together a summary.

Skill Focus

Identifying beginning, middle, and end of a story; summarizing main ideas, events, and themes; recalling significant details; classifying ideas

Materials & Resources

Text
- A story with easily identifiable story elements (Used in this lesson: "Little Red Riding Hood")

Other
- Transparency of Beginning, Middle, End Story Map (Appendix, p. 125)
- For each set of partners: 1 photocopy of same Map and 1 sheet of lined paper
- Fairy tale anthologies

Bonus Ideas

Have students create booklets like those on page 43 (but with three flaps). Have them write *beginning* on the first flap, *middle* on the next, and *end* on the third. On the backside of each flap, students should write a brief summary of that section of text. Under the flap, they should draw a picture that illustrates the same section.

STEPS

1. Discuss with the class the typical text structure used for virtually all narratives—quite simply, stories are usually told in a format of what happened in the beginning, what happened in the middle, and then what happened at the end. Folded within each of these segments are the story elements of character, setting, plot, problem, and solution. Tell students that the best way to summarize a narrative is to first map out its structure.

2. Display the Beginning, Middle, End Story Map transparency. Retell a familiar story or fairy tale, stopping periodically to sketch an element in the appropriate box and to write a description underneath—thus mapping the story line both graphically and verbally.

3. As you complete the first section (what happened in the beginning), point out that the beginning usually reveals the main character and the setting, and hints at the problem. For the next section (what happened in the middle), draw and fill in events to describe how the problem is fully revealed and how the rest of the plot unfolds. For the last section (what happened in the end), think aloud as you determine how the story's problem is resolved and sketch and record that. Complete this section with a description of the wrap-up of the story. Below are the elements that you would fill in for the sample story:

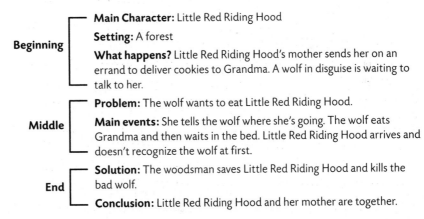

Beginning
- **Main Character:** Little Red Riding Hood
- **Setting:** A forest
- **What happens?** Little Red Riding Hood's mother sends her on an errand to deliver cookies to Grandma. A wolf in disguise is waiting to talk to her.

Middle
- **Problem:** The wolf wants to eat Little Red Riding Hood.
- **Main events:** She tells the wolf where she's going. The wolf eats Grandma and then waits in the bed. Little Red Riding Hood arrives and doesn't recognize the wolf at first.

End
- **Solution:** The woodsman saves Little Red Riding Hood and kills the bad wolf.
- **Conclusion:** Little Red Riding Hood and her mother are together.

4. Model how you look back through the completed story map and recombine the elements to create a concise summary of the whole story.

5. Set up partners. Distribute a lined sheet of paper and a Beginning, Middle, End Story Map to each partner group. Assign each a different fairy tale. Instruct students to work together to retell the story and to illustrate and fill in the elements appropriately. (Have available fairy tale anthologies that students can use for reference as needed.) Then have students use their story map to write a summary of the story.

CAPTIONS CAPTURE IT!

Prior to the Lesson: In your selected informational text, locate a page that includes both graphics and captions. For one caption, prepare an alternative that you'll be ready to use during the lesson. (You might deliberately make it quite different from and/or less or more effective than the original.) Use snipped sticky notes to cover all the captions on the page.

STEPS

1. Tell students that a book's graphics—including photographs, drawings, and diagrams—are an opportunity for the author to illustrate text points as well as to convey additional information. Explain that the captions, the concise descriptions that accompany the graphics, are actually summaries of important information. Good readers always study the visuals and captions carefully as they read.

2. Display the transparency. Point out that you have purposefully masked all the captions. Read the text aloud to students.

3. Model how you study a graphic and try to determine how it relates to the text on the page. Think aloud as you write a caption (use the space under the graphic or the margin).

4. List several questions on the board and challenge students to use the questions to evaluate your caption. Below are some questions you might use:

   - Does my caption match the picture?

   - Does it relate to the content of the text on the page?

   - Have I used the fewest words possible?

5. After the class has reached a consensus about your caption, remove the sticky note and compare yours to the author's. Invite students to decide which is more effective and discuss why.

6. Now, distribute a photocopy of the masked page to each student. Have students work individually or with partners. Ask them to write captions for the remaining graphics on the page. Remind students to refer to the three guiding questions you've written on the board.

7. Bring the class back together and call on different students or partners to share what they came up with. Have them explain how using the questions helped them write their captions.

LOOKING FOR THE MESSAGE THROUGH DIFFERENT EYES

Explanation

This lesson asks students to engage with a text in several different ways. It focuses their attention on yet another way to distill or summarize the main point in a story. It asks them to draw connections with their own lives and experiences. And, finally, it challenges them to look beyond the surface of a text and reminds them that literature is a way to reflect on life.

Skill Focus

Identifying the message or theme of text; summarizing main ideas, events, and themes in texts; recalling significant details in texts; categorizing and classifying ideas

Materials & Resources

Text

- Any grade-appropriate narrative text with clearly identifiable story elements and theme (Used in this lesson: *The Wednesday Surprise* by Eve Bunting)

Other

- Transparency or the chalkboard

Bonus Ideas

After this lesson, let students try their "eyes" with a new story. Either provide photocopies of a large-sized (full page) eye or have students sketch their own. Instruct them to use the interior of the eye to describe the message or deeper meaning in a story they've read. After they've shared their findings, post their "eye" messages in the hall for others to see.

STEPS

1. Tell students that one reason authors create stories is to give their readers something important and meaningful to think about. They hope their stories will help readers look carefully at things in their own lives and at their own views. Authors sometimes think of this as a *message* they want their readers to take away from their reading.

2. Explain that one good way to discover this message is first to find the main idea of the story. Good readers try to identify a story's core meaning or event and to summarize what the story is really all about. Then they can more easily discover what message the story holds for them and for their own lives.

3. Draw two pairs of large eyes on the board or on a transparency. Title one pair "Story's Eyes" and the other pair "My Eyes."

4. Read aloud the preselected text. Pose this question to the class:

   What was the main thing that happened in this story?

   For the sample story, a likely response might be:

   The granddaughter taught her grandmother to read as a surprise.

5. Point out that this statement is a kind of summary of the main point of the story. Write it under the "Story's Eyes" column. Then ask students to take a moment to think further about this summary statement. What message can they take away from it? Encourage them to use their own knowledge of life and their life's experiences to figure out a deeper meaning. Write their responses under the "My Eyes" column. An example list, based on the sample book, follows:

Story's Eyes	My Eyes
What the Story Is All About	**The Message I See in the Story**
The granddaughter taught her grandmother to read as a surprise.	Old people can learn from young people. You're never too old to stop learning.

6. Conclude by reminding students that even though a story isn't about their own lives, there might be a little surprise in it for them if they take time to think about what the story is really saying and how this might relate to their lives.

Using Text Features and Organizers

The manner in which text is organized, arranged, and presented to the reader is far from arbitrary. Especially in informational text, but in drama, poetry, and fiction as well, authors and editors purposefully include elements to help readers navigate texts. Too often, however, students of all ages overlook even obvious text signals. As teachers, we can address this situation by providing effective direct instruction in how to use these kinds of features.

Potentially helpful text signals abound. Books are divided into logical sections to help readers focus on specifics. Tables of contents and indexes help readers locate those specifics more efficiently so that they do not have to wade through pages of irrelevant material. Chapters, headings, and subheadings are provided to categorize and prioritize material. Special effects—such as boldfaced or italicized words, photo captions, or sidebar boxes—are also used to enhance presentation of important material.

In this section, you'll find lessons that focus on the text features and organizers most helpful to and appropriate for second and third graders. By these grade levels, the content load of the curriculum widens and deepens. Typically, students in these grades deal with numerous content areas—health, social studies, science, and math. Textbooks may be challenging for many students, filled with unfamiliar specialized content words and a demanding concept load. Narrative text also increases in complexity from what students encountered in first grade. Now they are expected to move beyond the basics of story structure to accomplish such sophisticated tasks as analyzing characters or grasping deeper nuances of drama and poetry.

For all these reasons, the lessons in this section provide students with pragmatic strategies they can put right to use to read more effectively. But because these students are, after all, still quite young, the lessons offer engaging and fun learning experiences. Students learn to differentiate the structure of fiction from nonfiction by setting up a "scientific" experiment, or they don costumes and "become" the parts of a book. They take an extended stroll through a scroll of informational text—experiencing, in a series of seven related lessons, how text features can help them better navigate and comprehend informational text. And, since testing is a reality of life even in these early grades, they learn the ins and outs and special language typical of many examinations. But even these lessons are nonthreatening—with teacher modeling, interaction, and hands-on examples built in to the structure of the lessons.

Knowing how to use text features helps this boy more easily locate a clue about a character's actions.

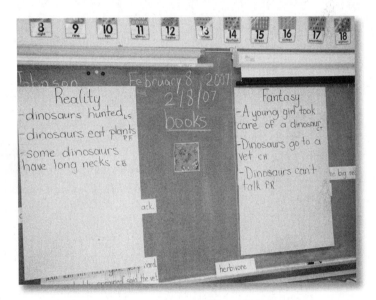

Because different genres are structured differently, learning to differentiate between them—as this class is doing—helps readers interact successfully with text.

Our goal throughout is to help students improve their reading and understanding by giving them a better grasp of the uniqueness of the many text structures and signals that are there to help them. We cannot assume that they will see the obvious. Our job, as in so much of education, is to help them find the way.

FICTION AND INFORMATIONAL TEXT: A BASIC DIFFERENCE

Explanation

This is a simple lesson about a simple concept. Nevertheless, it offers a core understanding for young students: Readers interact with different genres differently. The lesson is particularly engaging for primary-grade students because it invites them to participate in an "experiment" in which some of them act as researchers and others as experimenters.

Skill Focus

Distinguishing between fiction and nonfiction; identifying internal structure of text

Materials & Resources

Text

- Fiction books (enough for half the class)
- Informational books (enough for half the class)

Other

- Pencils and sheets of paper (enough for half the class)

STEPS

1. Tell students that today they will be conducting an experiment. Divide the class in half. Within each half, set up two groups. Designate one group as the experimenters and the other group as the researchers. Explain that each group has an equally important job: The experimenters will conduct the experiment while the researchers will observe the experiment and gather the information.

2. Call the two groups of researchers to one part of the room to meet with you. Distribute a sheet of paper and a pencil to each researcher. Tell them that the two groups of experimenters will be reading different genres—either fiction or nonfiction—but they won't know ahead of time what they're reading! Only the researchers will know. Explain that their job will be to carefully observe the experimenters and to make notes about their observations. You want them to pay special attention to these two criteria:

   - The speed at which the experimenters turn the pages: Do they do it slowly, with long pauses in between, or quite quickly and frequently?

   - The manner in which the experimenters turn the pages: Do they skip around as though they aren't reading everything or do they turn pages sequentially?

3. Next, distribute an assortment of fiction selections to one experimenters group. Give the other group of experimenters an assortment of informational books. (Don't identify, for either group, the genre you have handed out.) Instruct each group to enjoy reading these materials for ten minutes. Position the researchers groups near enough so that each can observe their respective experimenters closely.

4. When time is up, have the researchers share their notes and observations. Typical results will reveal that the fiction readers turned pages slowly in sequential order and that the informational text readers often flipped pages and didn't read in a certain sequence. If, for any reason, researchers have arrived at different conclusions, guide students to understand that these are typical behaviors for the two different genres.

5. Discuss with the class the conclusions that can be inferred from these observations: Good readers read fiction sequentially, from beginning to end, and they read informational text more randomly, skipping around until something interests them or they find what they're looking for. Invite the whole class to discuss why these observations pertain.

LEARNING THE PARTS OF A BOOK THROUGH DRAMA

Explanation

Students will have fun with this lesson. After all, who's ever heard of a talking Table of Contents? The lesson gives students a chance to become actors and learn about drama elements while at the same time gaining a unique perspective on the parts of a book.

Skill Focus

Identifying the title, author, and illustrator of a text; identifying elements of drama; identifying the characteristics of genres, such as drama; using simple reference materials to obtain information

Materials & Resources

Text
- Play script with characters who represent the parts of a book (Used in this lesson: original script, *Tommy's Homework* by Cheryl Sigmon)
- An assortment of informational books

Other
- Photocopies of the play script, 1 for each student
- Hole puncher
- Wide-tip markers
- For Parts of a Book costumes: 8 strips of butcher paper, each 1 yard long and approximately 18" wide; 16 12" pieces of string or yarn
- For Author, Illustrator, Seth, and Tommy costumes: 2 pieces 8" x 11 ½" cardstock; 4 24" pieces of string or yarn

Note: *Although we have not broken this lesson into parts, the lesson will need to span several days.*

STEPS

1. Tell students that in this lesson they'll become actors and costume designers! Explain that in order to be ready to portray the various characters in this play, students need to have a good understanding of the parts of an informational book and also of the responsibilities of the author and the illustrator. Hold up a few informational books and review the definitions of these key terms. Below is a set of definitions that you might write on the board or chart paper:

   - **Table of Contents:** A list of the main contents of a book by chapters and sections in the order in which they occur

   - **Glossary:** An alphabetical listing in the back of a book that comprises key words, their pronunciations, and their definitions

   - **Index:** An alphabetical listing in the back of a book that lists key words, and subtopics, of the book along with page numbers for the material

   - **Appendix:** Additional information supplied in the back of the book that is referenced in the text

   - **Author:** The person who writes the text of a book

   - **Illustrator:** The person who creates the drawings to accompany the text

2. Tell students that there is another set of terms and concepts they'll need to know before putting on this play—the elements of drama. Some of these may be review and others will be new. Just as you did in Step 1, create a list of key terms. As part of a class discussion of these terms, engage students in a comparison of drama elements and the parts of a book. An example list of terms, definitions, and comparisons follows:

   - **Act:** A major section in a play. Its role is much like a chapter in a book. There is likely a change in the action or a change in the setting for each act.

   - **Scene:** A part of an act that is often focused on one plot development and set in one place. It is much like a subheading in a chapter of a book.

   - **Script:** The story that the play tells. It is written in dialogue format to be spoken by actors. Each time a different character speaks, the script starts on a new line with that character's name. Although it contains almost *everything* of importance in a play, a script can be most easily likened to the dialogue in a book.

   - **Stage Directions:** They are an important part of a script because they tell actors what to do and how to move. These are usually written in italicized type within parentheses or brackets so that actors won't confuse them with their lines. They are similar to the action description in a novel or story.

- To make the costumes:

For the Parts of a Book: Punch 2 holes in the top of each of the 8 strips of the butcher paper. Thread the measured string/yarn through the holes and tie so that the actors' arms will fit through the loop. Write the book title, label the book parts, and position the strips to reflect whether they occur at the front or back of the book. See diagrams below.

For the Author, Illustrator, Seth, and Tommy: Cut a piece of cardstock in half widthwise. On one half write "Author" and on the other half write "Illustrator." Punch holes on the top sides of each and run a piece of string through the holes. Hang the card loosely around the necks of these two characters. See diagrams below.

Front View: Front parts of book · **Front View: Back parts of book**

Back View: All parts of book · **All Other Characters**

- **Playwright:** The person who writes a play. He or she is like the author of a book.

- **Costume Designers:** People who create the costumes for the actors. There is really nothing quite like them in books; however, when authors describe what their characters look like and wear, they are functioning as "costume designers" for the moment!

3. Once students are familiar with both sets of terms and concepts, introduce the play to the class. You might read it aloud once through or distribute individual copies of the script and ask students to read it.

4. Assign parts and allow students to practice reading their parts until they're fluent. They may need guidance for the first few rehearsals but should soon be able to practice independently.

5. Assign costume designers who should work, with your guidance, to create the costumes for the actors. Stress the importance and creativity involved in costume designing. Reassure these students that they are just as necessary to the overall production as the actors. "Behind the scenes" work in drama is always critical to the success of a performance and students need to understand this.

6. After students have practiced sufficiently and have become fluent, it's time to put on your production! You may want to send out invitations and invite another class to enjoy your play. Following is a script for an original play targeted for this lesson's instructional goals.

Tommy's Homework

Parts:

Tommy	Index
Seth, his friend	Table of Contents
Author	Glossary
Illustrator	Appendix

Act I

Scene I   *[two students walking home from school]*

Tommy   *[talking to himself]*: I've got so much homework tonight. I guess I'd better hurry home and get it done.

Seth: Hi, Tommy!

Tommy: Hi, Seth!

Seth: Where are you going?

Tommy: I have lots of homework, so I'm going home to get it all done.

Seth: That's too bad. I was hoping you could play baseball with Paul and me.

Tommy: Well, maybe I can play for a little while. I guess my homework can wait.

[They walk away to the ball field.]

Act I

Scene II *[two students leaving the ball field]*

Seth: Wow! We played ball all afternoon! I'm so tired!

Tommy: Oh! I didn't watch the time. I'd better run home and get to work on my homework.

Seth: See you tomorrow!

Tommy: Bye! I'll see you at school.

Act II

Scene I *[Tommy's bedroom]*

Tommy *[talking to himself]*: I'm supposed to answer these questions for homework. I think I'll study on the bed since I'm so tired. *[He lies on the bed with his book and yawns.]*

Tommy *[talking to himself]*: I sure wish I had help with these questions. Let me see. The first question is…

[He falls asleep on his bed.]

Act II

Scene II *[dream sequence: the book comes to life]*

Author: Hey, Tommy! *[He nudges Tommy, but Tommy doesn't move.]* How come you're sleeping? I'm the author of this book. I wrote it, and it's really exciting. It's all about earthquakes. You love to read about earthquakes, don't you? Wake up!

Illustrator: I'm the illustrator. I drew all of these great pictures. Surely they can keep you awake! Look at this one with hot lava spewing into the air! Wake up!

Author: Poor Tommy! He's just too tired. He said he needed help, and he was right.

Table of Contents, Glossary, Index, and Appendix: We can help him find the answers to his questions.

Illustrator: Let's see what the first question is: "How are earthquakes measured?"

Table of Contents: Hey! I can get us started. I have information about where all of the main topics are included. They're all in the order you'll find them in the book. I'm right in the front of the book. Let's look down my list for something to do with earthquakes.

[Illustrator looks up and down the Table of Contents.]

Illustrator: Here it is! There's a chapter called "What Causes Earthquakes," and one part is called "Earthquakes and How They Are Measured." That's just what Tommy needs! I'll write the answer for him. *[He takes a pencil and begins to write in Tommy's notebook.]*

Author: His next question is "What is a *seismograph?*" We could read the chapter and find out, or there's another quick way to find that answer. We need you, Glossary!

Glossary: Oh, goody! I want to help Tommy. Let's look in my list. I'm like a dictionary, but I only have important words from the chapters in this book. I have all of my words in alphabetical order to help you. I even tell you how to pronounce words if you don't know. I'm located in the back of the book. *[He looks down his list.]* Here's the word. *Seismograph* is an instrument that records earthquake waves and tells how strong they are. Author, write that down for Tommy!

[Author begins writing in Tommy's notebook.]

Illustrator: The next question says to look at the map in the Appendix on page 107 and find how many earthquakes are recorded in California each year. We need you, Appendix.

Appendix: I'm glad to help. I have lots of charts, graphs, maps, and other information for readers. I'm an extra treat for the reader. Usually your chapter will tell you the information I have that might add to what you know about a topic. I'm in the back of the book. Let's find out about earthquakes in California. *[He looks down at himself.]* Wow! Scientists record more than 30,000 earthquakes in California each year! Write that down, Author!

[Author records the answer in Tommy's notebook.]

Illustrator: Let's see what his next question is: "Why is the focus of an earthquake important?"

Table of Contents: Maybe I can tell you where to read about the focus of an earthquake. Look down my list and see.

[Glossary looks down his list.]

Glossary: I don't see anything about the focus of an earthquake. We know which chapter is about earthquakes. I guess we could read the chapter and look for the word *focus.*

Index: I'm Index, and I've got a better idea. I have lots of words from the chapters in me. I have all of my words in alphabetical order. I don't tell you the definitions of them, but I tell you on which page you can read about them. *[He looks down his list.]* You'll find the answer on page 13. You can go right to the page, and you don't have to read the whole chapter. I'll tell you exactly where to look. Isn't that cool? I can save you lots of time!

Table of Contents: Well, we can all save people time if they know how to use us and when to use us. Right?

All: Right!

Index, Glossary, and Appendix: People just have to remember to look in the back of the book for us!

Table of Contents: Don't forget me, too! I'm right in the front of the book.

[Tommy begins to wake up. He stretches and yawns.]

Index: Hurry! We'd better get back in the book!

[The book parts hide.]

Act II

Scene III *[Tommy wakes up.]*

Tommy: Oh, I must have fallen asleep. I'll never get this homework finished for tomorrow! *[He picks up his notebook and looks surprised.]* How in the world did I get all this work done in my sleep? It's like I had lots of help, but how could that be? *[He scratches his head.]* I'll have to do more of my homework in my sleep!

TWO-PART LESSON: TEST TEXT AS A GENRE

PART 1: WHERE LITTLE WORDS ARE IMPORTANT

"Teaching to the test" has long had negative connotations. In addition, many teachers avoid teaching test taking because they fear criticism for somehow breaching test security. However, testing is a fact of life. There are legitimate ways to use sample questions (often provided by the states themselves) to offer students a genuine test-taking experience. And teaching the vocabulary, organization, and conditions of testing is not "teaching to the test," but instead simply familiarizing students with the reality of what they will ultimately be held accountable for. In this two-lesson series, you'll find suggestions for providing students with sample questions as well as for giving them real-life experience with testing language and expectations.

···O **Skill Focus**

Practicing test-like questions; responding to questions of *who, what, why, when, where* and asking to clarify unclear areas; establishing purposes for reading

···O **Materials & Resources**

Text

- Sample multiple-choice test questions (either sample items from your state schools' Web site or original questions that you generate based on your state's examples)

Other

- A transparency of several sample multiple-choice test questions

- For each student: 1 photocopy of similar questions

Prior to the Lesson: Check your state schools' Web site for information about test materials. Become familiar with the rubrics used to score your state's exams and the conditions that are advertised to the public. Many states also offer sample test items online. (If your state doesn't offer sample items, check out another state's Web site where sample items are available and/or generate your own questions based on the information your state does provide.) Without copying the referenced text, make a sheet of questions for your students. In addition to this sheet, create a transparency of representative questions for modeling. Be sure that key words such as those that follow are included in the questions you use: who, what, why, when, where, how, how much, how long, always, never, sometimes, no, not, all, every, best, some, many, might, can, may.

STEPS

1. Inform students that test taking does not have to be mysterious or intimidating. There are secrets that everyone can learn to make the whole process a lot easier and smoother. Since students will be involved in an increasing amount of test taking as they progress through the grades, it's time that they started learning some of those secrets. Today, they will learn how to pay close attention to *every* word in the questions they're asked.

2. Display the transparency you've prepared. Model for students how you read each question and search for all important words. Explain that important words include those words that tell exactly what the test taker is supposed to be looking for. Circle these words. Demonstrate, too, how you look out for general, everyday words that are key clues to the focus of the question. Underline these words. Make sure students realize that neither of these categories includes content words. (Note that although this lesson focuses on multiple-choice questions, it applies as well to short or long written-response questions.) Below are two examples of test directions and/or questions, with a sample teacher commentary:

The (best) choice for a title for this story would be:

Explain: "Boys and girls, I circled the word *best* because it is the important word here. It tells us exactly what is wanted: There might be more than one correct answer, but only the one that is considered the *best* choice is the right answer. I underlined the words *title* and *story* because they give me key clues about what I'm looking for (the title) and where I'm looking (in the story)."

Which direction is (not) the one Charles should choose?

Explain: "The word *not* is extremely important. It means three of the answers are directions he could successfully choose but only one direction does not work. It's the one that does not work that is the right answer here. So I circled *not*. Also, I underlined the word *direction* because that's the key clue about what Charles needs."

TWO-PART LESSON: TEST TEXT AS A GENRE

PART 2: ANSWERING THE WHOLE QUESTION

Explanation

In a very real sense, test text is in a category of its own, with special features and elements. This lesson continues teaching test-taking "savvy" that your students need. It focuses on another common and tricky test feature—multiple parts to questions. This feature applies especially to short and long written-response test questions.

Skill Focus

Practicing test-like questions; responding to questions of *who, what, why, when, where* and asking to clarify unclear areas; establishing purposes for reading

Materials & Resources

Text

- Sample short or long written-response test questions (either sample items from your state schools' Web site or original questions that you generate based on your state's examples)

Other

- A transparency of several sample short or long written-response test questions

- For each student: 1 photocopy of similar questions

Bonus Ideas

Let students practice the art of forming questions using some of the "little words" so important in test questions. Have them rephrase the headings and subheadings of a chapter of content material. For example, "Building Communities" becomes "How are communities built?"

Note: See "Prior to the Lesson" on page 107.

STEPS

1. Review with students what they learned in Part 1 of this lesson: They need to read every word in a test question, search for important and key clue words, and circle and underline those words. Explain that today you'll focus on a different kind of test-taking secret they need to know. Sometimes questions have more than one part. This is especially true of questions that ask for written responses. Tell students that successful test takers read extremely carefully to discover how many items their response should address.

2. Display the transparency you've prepared. Model for students how you read the questions carefully. Think aloud about how many parts each question includes and about exactly what you need to do to respond to those different parts. Underline and number the different items you must respond to. Below are two examples of test questions and directions, with a sample teacher commentary:

   <u>Why was Doreen unhappy about her lost book?</u> (#1) <u>Tell how you know this.</u> (#2)

   Explain: "Boys and girls, this test question could be tricky, but I'm not going to be tricked! If I look really carefully, I can see that it has two parts. First there's a question about why Doreen is unhappy. If I answer that question, I might think I'm done. But I'm not. There's a second part that is just as important. In this part, I have to tell why I believe what I said about Doreen. I need to defend my answer with examples from the text. I need to read carefully and include whatever information I can find that will support my answer. If I skipped this second part, I wouldn't have answered this question successfully."

   <u>Tell why Tony wanted the teacher to outlaw homework</u> (#1) and <u>tell what you think he should do about it</u> (#2).

   Explain: "When I read this question, I see that it has the word *and* in the middle of the prompt and that it repeats the word *tell*. So I know right away that there are two things I need to do in order to fully answer the question. I've first got to use the text to tell the reasons Tony wanted the teacher to outlaw homework. But if I answer just this first part, I won't be done. I'm also asked to tell my own thoughts about what Tony should do. That part is my opinion, but it needs to make sense according to what I've read in the story. And it's just as important as the first part."

3. Now distribute a sheet of questions to each student. Have them work individually and follow your model in answering the questions. Instruct them to underline and number as you have done. Afterward, discuss the questions with the class and guide them as necessary to understand the correct way to analyze the questions.

INFORMATIONAL TEXT: THE QUICK FIVE-STEP PREVIEW

STEPS

1. Tell students that today they will learn a previewing strategy with five quick steps. It provides an efficient method for previewing any informational text they're about to read, and it will increase their comprehension.

2. Mount a blank sheet of chart paper or posterboard. Title it "Quick 5-Step Previewing Strategy." List the five steps shown below:

Quick 5-Step Previewing Strategy
(Where you see [?], ask yourself, "How does this connect to the topic?")
1. Look at the title/topic and ask yourself what you already know about it.
2. Look at the headings and subheadings. [?]
3. Look at the key words that are underlined, boldfaced, or in color. [?]
4. Look at the graphics (photos, illustrations, charts, graphs). [?]
5. Look at the beginning and ending. [?]

3. Display the preselected text and announce the topic. Then model how you think aloud about any background knowledge you already have about the topic. For example, with the sample book you might say, "Okay, the topic is bald eagles. I think I know a few things about this subject. Let's see, I know the bald eagle is on many of our coins and is a symbol for the U.S. Post Office. It seems to represent a lot about our country. I've even been lucky enough to see a bald eagle flying, and they're really majestic."

4. Thumb through the book and examine the headings and subheadings. Read each aloud and ask, "Now, how does this connect to the topic?" and attempt to answer the question. For example, for the chapter in the sample book titled "A Threatened Species," you might share, "I know that the bald eagle is still a threatened bird and is protected from being hunted by people, but I can't remember if it's still endangered. I hope I'll find out."

5. Model how you look through the text to find highlighted words, including words that are boldfaced, in color, or underlined. As you say each word, repeat, "How does this connect to the topic?" and make your best guess.

6. Now skim through to locate the book's visual aids—charts, graphs, photos, illustrations—and with each one repeat, "How does this connect to the topic?" Try to make a reasonable connection to the topic in order to provide a good model for students.

7. Finally, read the chapter's beginning and ending paragraphs. Point out how they give the "big picture" idea explored in this chapter.

8. Conclude by telling students, "I think I have a good idea about this chapter. Now I can read it and fill in any gaps in my thinking."

Explanation

Students need to learn the features of informational text that are designed to help them organize, prioritize, and understand the content. This lesson teaches students some steps for previewing text using these features. If students internalize these steps and put them to use automatically as they start informational text chapters, they will increase their comprehension without even realizing it!

Skill Focus

Explaining steps/following steps in a process; identifying the characteristics of genres; using simple reference materials to obtain information

Materials & Resources

Text

- A grade-appropriate, informational text with chapter headings and with highlighted key words (Used in this lesson: *The Bald Eagle* by Patricia Ryon Quiri)

Other

- Posterboard or chart paper

Bonus Ideas

Because this is such a helpful strategy, you might want to retain the poster you create in Step 3 as a permanent classroom display chart. Remind students to refer to it for future informational text reading assignments.

SEVEN-PART LESSON: SCROLLING FOR TEXT FEATURES

PART 1: THE BIGGEST WORDS ARE THE TOPIC

Explanation

Students' awareness of text features can be the critical difference between successful or compromised text comprehension. This lesson is the first in an extended series of lessons that look in depth at key text features. Presenting text in a scroll fashion, as these lessons do, provides a clear and fun way for students to understand the way the text signals work and to grasp relationships among features.

Skill Focus

Distinguishing between fiction and nonfiction; using simple reference materials to obtain information; identifying the characteristics of informational texts

Materials & Resources

Text

- For modeling: A chapter of a content area textbook that has a clear title, chapter headings and subheadings, an identifiable overview/introduction, highlighted words, signal words, graphics with captions, and an effective summary (Used in this lesson series: the chapter "What Are Rocks?" from *Earth Science*, Harcourt Science)

- For students' work: a comparable content area textbook chapter

Other

- Text scrolls (see "Prior to the Lesson" note)

- For each student: 1 photocopy of Text Signals Chart (Appendix, p. 126); a ruler; 1 sheet of paper

Prior to the Lesson: Photocopy the textbook chapter you've selected for student use. Make one copy for each partner or small group. Use tape to join the text pages. To create the effect of a scroll, join the pages at the sides, rather than top to bottom.

STEPS

1. Explain to students that authors, illustrators, editors, and publishers, create many aids to help readers navigate their way through informational text. But in order for these aids to be of any real use, they have to be noticed and understood. Tell students that they're about to embark on an extended series of lessons that will teach them how to work with seven different important text signals. Today's lesson focuses on how text formatting provides clues about the relative significance of information and ideas.

2. Set up small groups or partners. (Take into consideration the fact that the same groups will need to work together for seven lessons.) Distribute one scroll to each partner set or group and a photocopy of the Text Signals Chart (Appendix, p. 126) to each student. Instruct students to fold the chart in half three times and then unfold it so that the page now has eight divisions.

3. Write the term *type size* on the board. Tell students that editors and publishers use various type sizes to signal readers about what's important and what's less important in a text selection. If readers really pay attention, they'll find quite an assortment of different-size type in informational text.

4. Distribute a ruler and a sheet of paper to each student. Have groups roll out their scrolls on the floor and invite them to stretch out along the scroll. Direct them to explore several pages but not to focus on what the text says. Instead, they should pay attention to the different uses and sizes of type. Have them measure the height of the different letters they discover and record their measurements, along with the page number and a few example words in each text size. (This is a good math activity, too!) Bring the class back together and have each group share a few different examples.

5. Now bring students' attention to the largest print in the chapter you're using for modeling: the title. Point out that a chapter's title usually expresses the biggest idea—in fact, it indicates the umbrella idea, or topic, for the whole chapter—and for that reason it is shown in the biggest print. For example, for the sample text, the chapter title is "What Are Rocks?" and the topic is "Rocks."

6. Have students use the first box on their Text Signals Charts to record the title for the chapter on their scrolls. They should use that same box to fill in the topic. Ask them to brainstorm what they already know about this topic and record it in the chart's first section, under the chapter title.

Seven-Part Lesson: Scrolling for Text Features

Part 2: Headings and Subheadings Are Next

Explanation

In this lesson, students continue their journey through their text scrolls. They pick up from the previous lesson and search again for type of varying sizes—this time focusing on headings and subheadings. They need to understand that these signals have been provided to help them prioritize information. The lesson also includes an opportunity for students to outline the topic, headings, and subheadings and thus to visualize the text's hierarchy in an additional way.

Skill Focus

Distinguishing between fiction and nonfiction; using simple reference materials to obtain information; identifying the characteristics of informational texts

Materials & Resources

Text

- For modeling: Same text used in Part 1 of this lesson (Used in this lesson series: the chapter "What Are Rocks?" from *Earth Science*, Harcourt Science)

- For students' work: comparable content area textbook chapter used in Part 1

Other

- Students' text scrolls from Part 1 of this lesson

- Highlighters or crayons in assorted colors

- Students' Text Signals Charts (Appendix, p. 126) from Part 1

Steps

1. Review with the class what they learned in Part 1: An informational text uses varying type size to signify the relative importance of ideas. Confirm that students learned specifically that the largest type size in a chapter is usually the chapter's title, which also reveals the biggest idea, or topic.

2. Explain that today you will continue in the same vein, examining the next several levels of chapter headings. In descending order by type size, these will indicate tiers of importance of subtopics covered in the chapter. Display the chapter you're using for modeling and show students how you locate a few headings. For example, for the sample text, you would identify the headings "Identifying Rocks" and "Types of Rocks." Go on to model how you find the subheadings. Remind students that you are now looking for a smaller-size heading. For the sample text, under "Types of Rocks," you would locate these three subheadings: "Igneous Rocks," "Sedimentary Rocks," and "Metamorphic Rocks." (You might also point out that not all sections have subheadings.)

3. On a transparency or the board, list the headings and subheadings as an outline. An example for the sample book is at right. Think aloud about what you might expect to find in each of these sections, what their relationship is to the umbrella topic, and how they relate to one another.

What Are Rocks?

Identifying Rocks

Types of Rocks

  Igneous Rocks

   Sedimentary Rocks

    Metamorphic Rocks

4. Distribute scrolls and Text Signals Charts. Have partners or groups follow your model and work their way through the scroll to locate all headings and subheadings. Instruct them to use a different-colored marker (from the color used for the title) to circle the headings and a marker in yet another color to circle the subheadings. Remind them to be careful: All type circled in a particular color must be of the same size.

5. Now ask students to list the headings and subheadings in outline style in the appropriate box on their charts. Allow time for partners or groups to discuss the relationships among and between the topic, headings, and subheadings.

SEVEN-PART LESSON: SCROLLING FOR TEXT FEATURES

PART 3: THE BEGINNING TELLS THE BIG IDEA

Explanation

In the third lesson in this "scrolling" series, students begin to delve into reading the text. The focus here is on a chapter's introduction, which presents the chapter's main idea and offers a brief overview of what's to come in the text. Readers need to make use of this introduction so they can better focus their reading of the rest of the chapter.

Skill Focus

Distinguishing between fiction and nonfiction; using simple reference materials to obtain information; identifying the characteristics of informational texts; summarizing main ideas

Materials & Resources

Text

- For modeling: Same text used in previous parts of this lesson (Used in this lesson series: the chapter "What Are Rocks?" from *Earth Science*, Harcourt Science)

- For students' work: textbook chapter used in previous parts

Other

- Students' text scrolls from previous parts

- Highlighters or crayons in assorted colors

- Students' Text Signals Charts (Appendix, p. 126) from previous parts

STEPS

1. Review students' learning from Parts 1 and 2 of this lesson: An informational text uses varying type size to signify the relative importance of ideas. Discuss with students the hierarchy of ideas that moves from title/topic to headings to subheadings.

2. Tell students that the feature you'll focus on today will involve their actually starting to read, rather than skim through, the selection. They'll start at the likely place—the beginning, or introduction. Explain that a chapter's introductory section usually provides an overview of what the chapter will contain. It is a concise and condensed description of the main, or big, idea that the chapter will explore.

3. Display the chapter you're using for modeling and read aloud its introduction. Point out explicitly how it acts as a brief overview for the chapter and model how you rephrase the big idea in your own words. For example, for the sample chapter, you might say, "This paragraph states that the chapter will investigate how rocks are identified and classified by the different ways they form. That's the big idea—it's a little more specific than the title and it shows how the two headings relate. You should always read the beginning paragraph or section carefully for this kind of overview. It prepares you for the rest of the chapter."

4. Distribute scrolls and Text Signals Charts. Have partners or groups follow your model to locate and read the chapter's introductory section.

5. Ask them to rephrase the big idea in their own words and to record that in the third box on their charts. Encourage them to keep their descriptions brief—space is quite limited on the chart and this will give them good practice in distilling ideas and writing concisely.

PART 4: OUTSTANDING WORDS

Explanation

In the fourth lesson in this series, the focus shifts to special words. Young readers don't automatically realize that highlighted words are called out because they are particularly significant, or key, words. But once clued in to this feature, students can easily spot the words and learn to give them extra attention.

Skill Focus

Distinguishing between fiction and nonfiction; using simple reference materials to obtain information; identifying the characteristics of informational texts; summarizing main ideas; using content/specialized words

Materials & Resources

Text

- For modeling: Same text used in previous parts of this lesson (Used in this lesson series: the chapter "What Are Rocks?" from *Earth Science*, Harcourt Science)

- For students' work: textbook chapter used in previous parts

Other

- Students' text scrolls; highlighters or crayons

- Students' Text Signals Charts (Appendix, p. 126)

Note: *At about this point in the process, it's helpful to start a classroom display chart of the text features that students are learning. Each day you can jot down the signal you've covered in that lesson, along with a brief definition and example.*

STEPS

1. Review students' learning from the previous three lessons in this series. By now they've become aware of type size, chapter hierarchy, and introduction. In addition to keeping an ongoing display chart listing text features, it might also be helpful to tack up different groups' scrolls each day. A student from the chosen group can come forward to identify features the class has already learned.

2. Explain to students that today's lesson focuses on key terms. You might tell them that you think of these as "outstanding words" because they literally stand out from the rest of the text. Authors, editors, and publishers provide signals such as color, underlining, italics, or boldfacing to make sure readers realize these words are special. (Note: You might also want to point out that sometimes ordinary words are highlighted, usually for design or graphic purposes. Be sure to reinforce, however, that highlighting is typically used for key terms, so students are always wise to pay attention to it.)

3. Display the chapter you're using for modeling and flip through the pages to note several highlighted words. Model how you analyze these words and figure out how they might help you understand the chapter. For example, for the sample book, you might say, "Here's an outstanding word. It's the word pressure. Let me think how this word might connect to the topic. I think it might relate to rocks because pressure helps to form certain rocks. I can see how that would be a key word."

4. Now, have students form their groups or partner sets. Distribute their scrolls and Text Signals Charts. Instruct them to circle all the words that the author and publisher have called out in some special way. Afterward, they should list several of the words in the "Key Words" section on their charts.

5. Finally, have groups discuss how they feel the word might relate to the topic.

SEVEN-PART LESSON: SCROLLING FOR TEXT FEATURES

PART 5: SIGNAL WORDS

Explanation

By this fifth lesson in the scrolling series, students have already become familiar with an impressive repertoire of text features. Here they continue to work with special words, but this kind, called *signal words*, are more challenging because they are not called out in print. Students need to learn to be keen observers of text to find these organizers.

Skill Focus

Distinguishing between fiction and nonfiction; using simple reference materials to obtain information; identifying the characteristics of informational texts; summarizing main ideas; using content/specialized words

Materials & Resources

Text

- For modeling: Same text used in previous parts of this lesson (Used in this lesson series: the chapter "What Are Rocks?" from *Earth Science*, Harcourt Science)

- For students' work: textbook chapter used in previous parts

Other

- Students' text scrolls from previous parts

- Highlighters or crayons in assorted colors

- Students' Text Signals Charts (Appendix, p. 126) from previous parts

STEPS

1. Briefly review with the class what they have learned from the previous four lessons—relation of type size to title/topic and chapter hierarchy, and the role of the introduction and highlighted key words. Refer to the display chart if you are using this, and/or invite one group to tack up their scroll and use it to identify features the class has already learned.

2. Tell students that today's lesson will again call attention to important words. However, these words—called *signal words*—are different from the outstanding key words they've already studied. Although some signal words are boldfaced (especially those that summarize a selection), they are typically not highlighted and look just like regular text. This makes them a lot trickier to find! Good readers know they need to scan the text carefully to find them.

3. Tell students that signal words are different from key words in another way. They don't themselves convey important concepts or ideas; instead they call attention to the text structure or flow. Their job is literally to signal readers about something worth noting or remembering. List common signal words on the board. A sample list follows:

Most importantly	First	Second	In addition
In conclusion	Next	Third [and subsequent numbers]	In summary
Finally	Last	Interestingly	To summarize

4. Display the chapter you're using for modeling and show students how you skim to find signal words. Point out that they usually occur at the beginnings and endings of text sections. For example, for the sample book, you might think aloud, "Hmm. . . I see that this paragraph starts with 'Most importantly,' so I know I need to pay close attention to what comes after these words. The paragraph tells me that the way rocks are formed reveals what type of rocks they are. I'll need to remember that."

5. Now have students form their groups or partner sets. Distribute their scrolls and Text Signals Charts. Instruct them to skim carefully and to circle or highlight all the signal words that they find. Afterward, they should list these words, along with the appropriate page numbers, in the appropriate box on their charts.

6. To bring closure, ask different groups to share what they found. If you're constructing an ongoing chart for the class, add this feature to the list.

SEVEN-PART LESSON: SCROLLING FOR TEXT FEATURES

PART 6: GRAPHICS AND CAPTIONS

Explanation

Students' scrolling continues as they focus in this lesson on reading graphics and captions. This lesson helps them realize that information can be given in many different ways and visuals are sometimes the best format. They need to learn to read visuals and captions just as they do the main body of the text.

Skill Focus

Identifying and using graphic representations such as charts, graphs, pictures, and graphic organizers; distinguishing between fiction and nonfiction; using simple reference materials to obtain information; identifying the characteristics of informational texts; summarizing main ideas

Materials & Resources

Text

- For modeling: Same text used in previous parts of this lesson (Used in this lesson series: the chapter "What Are Rocks?" from *Earth Science*, Harcourt Science)

- For students' work: textbook chapter used in previous parts

Other

- Students' text scrolls from previous parts

- Highlighters or crayons in assorted colors

- Students' Text Signals Charts (Appendix, p. 126) from previous parts

STEPS

1. Briefly review with the class what they have learned from the previous five lessons in this series. Refer to the display chart if you are using this, and/or have one group tack up their scroll and use it to identify features the class has already learned.

2. Now ask students if they have ever heard the adage "A picture is worth a thousand words." Ask a volunteer(s) to explain what it might mean. Confirm that often a picture can say something quickly and more clearly than lots of words.

3. Explain that pictures are used in text materials not just for decoration—they play an important role in conveying information. Ask students to help you brainstorm different kinds of text graphics. List these on the board. Be sure the list includes items such as photographs, charts, diagrams, graphs, maps, and drawings.

4. Display the chapter you're using for modeling and flip through the pages to locate different visuals. On the board list, check off each item you find.

5. Now write the word *caption* on the board. Explain that graphics usually have captions to summarize what is being illustrated. Captions are written next to or below the illustrations. Refer again to the model chapter and call attention to the captions. Tell students that good readers try to read and interpret graphics on their own but they also use captions to confirm and enhance their understanding.

6. Finally, select a few of the visuals in the chapter and think aloud as you connect them to the overall topic. For example, for the sample book, you might say, "All illustrations in an informational text chapter should relate in some way to the chapter's topic. This diagram shows layers of earth. The arrows pointing down must represent pressure on these layers. How do I think it connects to the topic? I think this shows how the earth compresses and forms this rock. Let me check the caption, too. The caption says, 'Heat and pressure can change the metamorphic rock into another type of metamorphic rock.' So, I'm glad I read that because, although I had made the connection about how rocks form, I got some additional information from the caption."

7. Now have students form their groups or partner sets. Distribute their scrolls and Text Signals Charts. Instruct them to look through their scrolls to locate graphics. Have them draw a border around each graphic and accompanying caption that they find. They should then use the appropriate boxes on their Text Signals Charts to record the types of visuals they've found. Finally, have groups discuss how the visuals and captions relate to the overall topic.

SEVEN-PART LESSON: SCROLLING FOR TEXT FEATURES

PART 7: THE END IS THE BIG PICTURE AGAIN

Explanation

With this lesson, students arrive at the end of their scrolling work. They end with a suitable feature—the ending of the chapter. Just as a chapter typically begins with an introduction that reveals the main idea of the text to follow, it usually concludes with a summary that ties everything up. And that is what students will do today!

Skill Focus

Distinguishing between fiction and nonfiction; using simple reference materials to obtain information; identifying the characteristics of informational texts; summarizing main ideas

Materials & Resources

Text

• For modeling: Same text used in previous parts of this lesson (Used in this lesson series: the chapter "What Are Rocks?" from *Earth Science*, Harcourt Science)

• For students' work: textbook chapter used in previous parts

Other

• Students' text scrolls from previous parts

• Highlighters or crayons in assorted colors

• Students' Text Signals Charts (Appendix, p. 126) from previous parts

STEPS

1. Discuss with students how much they've learned by now about text features. Briefly review the text features they've learned thus far—relation of type size to title/topic and chapter hierarchy, and the role of the introduction, highlighted key words, text signal words, and graphics and captions. Refer to the display chart if you are using this, and/or invite one group to tack up their scroll and use it to identify features the class has already learned.

2. Tell students that today's lesson presents the final text feature they'll be learning in this series. Ask them to think for a moment about the chapter introduction. Discuss how it opened the chapter with an overview of the big idea. Inform students that at the other end of the chapter—the conclusion—authors and editors include a similar feature. It's a summary and it is often even titled "Summary" or "Conclusion," so it's very easy to find! Point out that a summary is often written as one or more paragraphs but sometimes it is presented in a different format, such as a bulleted list or a set of reflective questions.

3. Display the book you're using for modeling and turn to the chapter's summary. Read it aloud and rephrase it in your own words. For example, for the sample book, you might say, "This summary tells me that rocks are made of minerals, and they're classified by the way they form. It reviews that we learned about three types: igneous rocks from cooled lava; sedimentary rocks from pieces of rock stuck together; and metamorphic rocks from heat and pressure. As I think about it, I realize this paragraph sums up the whole chapter!"

4. Now model how you think back to the chapter's introduction. Compare the summary with what you discovered there to be the big idea. For most well-constructed texts, you'll find that both the beginning and ending summarize the big idea of the entire text selection.

5. Have students form their groups or partner sets. Distribute their scrolls and Text Signals Charts. Instruct them to locate the conclusion of the chapter on their scrolls and to examine the specific way their text brings the chapter to an end. Have students read this summary and use the appropriate box on their Text Signals Charts to describe the summary in their own words.

6. Invite students to compare what they wrote on their charts for the introduction with what they have now written for the summary. Have some students share aloud with the class.

CHRONOLOGICAL ORDER HELPS NARRATIVES MAKE SENSE

Explanation

Students have worked with sequence before but the concept is so fundamental to narrative structure that this review will be valuable. And in addition, in this lesson they get to learn a big new word for the concept—*chronological*—as they reconnect the pieces of a story.

Skill Focus

Recalling details in a logical sequence; identifying characters, setting, and plot in a literary work; distinguishing between fiction and nonfiction; identifying internal structure of text

Materials & Resources

Text

- Multiple copies of a grade-appropriate narrative text with a clear sequence of events (Used in this lesson: *The Wednesday Surprise* by Eve Bunting)

Other

- Photocopies, 1 for each partner set or small group, of the list of story events (as prepared in "Prior to the Lesson")

Bonus Ideas

To extend this lesson, have students reposition the last event of the story to the top of the list. Ask if students think stories could ever start with the ending. Reveal that this is actually a technique that writers call "flashback." With the flashback technique, writers use the ending as a "hook" to draw in readers or viewers. Discuss some stories you've read in class and challenge students to consider whether the flashback technique could possibly work for them. Sometimes revealing the ending isn't a good idea!

Prior to the Lesson: Select about a dozen key events from the story you're using. Type or write a list of these events on a sheet of paper and snip the paper as shown at right. Make photocopies (one for each partner set or small group).

STEPS

1. Briefly review the concept of sequence and the words *sequence* and *sequential*, which should be familiar to most students. Explain that in today's lesson the class will learn a very big word that has the same meaning. The word is *chronological*.

2. Write *chronological* on the board. Underline the syllable *chron-*. Tell students that this word part means "time." Write *chron-* = time.

3. Explain that most narratives are written in chronological order. Help students to define that this means narratives are most often told in the time order in which they take place. (You might note that there are exceptions. See Bonus Ideas for one common exception.)

4. Invite students to create a chronological list. You might say, "Let's list what we've done so far today in chronological order." A sample list follows:

   1) We had our carpet time.
   2) We worked on math.
   3) We went to music.
   4) We had a short break for the restroom.
   5) Now we are in our guided reading time.

5. Organize partners or small groups. Distribute one or two copies of the preselected story to each partner set or group and instruct them to read the story. Tell students to pay careful attention to the order of the story's events.

6. Now distribute a photocopy of the list you've created. Show students how to pull apart the snipped sentences to make separate sentence strips. Instruct the groups or partners to work together to reconstruct the story's chronological order by laying out the strips on their desks.

7. Invite groups to share their chronologies. Have them discuss whether the story would make sense if the events were ordered differently.

Grandma arrives, and they have supper.

Everyone greets him with "Happy Birthday!"

Anna waits for her grandma to come to babysit on Wednesday night.

Grandma sits and reads to them.

She tells them that Anna taught her to read on Wednesdays!

When Dad rests, the family prepares for his party.

When Sam leaves, Anna and Grandma read together for a long time.

Dad comes home from work on Saturday.

Grandma leaves when Sam and Mom come home.

She says she may read everything in the world!

There is one more present from Grandma.

They open presents.

WHAT MAKES IT POETRY?

Explanation

Poetry offers unique opportunities to study text structure. Because it can take so many different creative forms, you can use it to demonstrate several important points in one lesson. Here, students learn how the main idea expressed in a prose selection can be interpreted in four quite different poetic variations, each one of them completely transformed from the original prose. And at the same time, they have a chance to consider just what it is about poetry that makes it unique!

Skill Focus

Identifying the characteristics of genres such as poetry; recognizing rhymes, rhythm, and patterned structures in children's texts, including poetry; responding to text in a variety of methods; identifying how the same topic is treated differently by various genres

Materials & Resources

Text
- Any grade-appropriate fiction or nonfiction selection (Used in this lesson: *Two Bad Ants* by Chris Van Allsburg)

Other
- Transparency or chalkboard

Bonus Ideas

Have students try writing a poem about something they've read in prose format. Encourage them to include as much of the content from the prose as possible.

STEPS

1. Discuss with students that writers find many different ways to express their ideas. Some write short stories, some write novels, some plays, and others poems. Ask the class if they can tell you—from their own reading experience—which of those formats typically offers the briefest way to express a writer's ideas. Guide them as necessary to see that poetry allows writers to communicate ideas—even important or complicated ones—in the fewest number of words possible.

2. Tell students that you're going to model the differences between the formats in a special way: You'll take the basic idea of a short story and transform it into a poem—in fact, into several different poems. Read aloud the preselected text. Then use a transparency or the chalkboard to present poetic versions of the same story line. Below are three example poems based on the sample book (identifying characteristics are shown in parentheses):

Poem #1 (short, rhyming)
Two bad ants
Decided not to return
So they ended in a coffee cup
With many things to learn!

Poem #2 (acrostic, unrhymed)
Always looking for a better life
Not seeing that theirs is good
Traveling into cups, water, and toasters
Soon came happily home!

Poem #3 (rhyming, shape poem—it changes directions to reflect the ants' movements)
Two bad ants
Went marching in a line
If only they had stayed in it
They would have been just fine!
But instead they went their own way
And with danger they took a chance
But at the end they fell in line
And became two good ants!

3. Discuss the different features of these simple poems. In addition to the identifying characteristics already provided, what do students notice about each? List appropriate features next to each poem.

4. Now, ask students to consider how poems differ from stories in the way they tell their message. Among the discussion points, include:

- Poems are not usually in complete sentences.
- Poems are extremely brief.
- Poems can be written in shapes.
- Poems don't have to have standard punctuation.
- Poems can rhyme.
- Poems can have rhythm.

Bookmarks

Did you choose the right book?

Ask yourself these questions. If your answer is "yes," the book is probably . . .

Too Hard

Is this an unfamiliar topic?
Are you confused about what's happening?
Are there many hard words?
When you read, does it sound choppy?
Do you find you're not enjoying this book?

Just Right

Is the book new to you?
Do you understand most of the book?
Are there a few new words?
When you read, is it mostly smooth?
Do you have to think as you read?

Too Easy

Have you read it lots of times before?
Do you understand the story really well?
Do you know almost every word?
Can you read it smoothly?
Are you reading without thinking?

---

c-a-t

Put your finger on the word and say all of the letters.

Use the picture clues.

th-ing

Look for parts you know.

The cat has 9 lives

Put your finger on the word and read the sentence.

sat fat
b<u>a</u>t m<u>a</u>t

Look for a rhyme you know.

3-Step Smart Guess

Approach it as a smart-guess word.

I Bet!

Looking at the title and cover, I bet	True	False	Page

Looking at the big print, I bet			

Looking at the pictures and charts, I bet			

I Bet!

Here are new things that I learned:	Should I have predicted this?		Page
	Yes	No	
	Yes	No	
	Yes	No	
	Yes	No	
	Yes	No	
	Yes	No	
	Yes	No	
	Yes	No	
	Yes	No	
	Yes	No	
	Yes	No	
	Yes	No	
	Yes	No	

Story Map

Characters	Main:	Other:
Setting		
Problem		
PLOT — Event		
Event		
Event		
Event		
Event		
Solution		
Ending		

Text Comparison Chart

Story Element of _____ in Text #1	How They Are Similar	Story Element of _____ in Text #2

Artist's Storyboard

Here's how I picture the main character . . .	Here's how I see the setting . . .	Here's the problem . . .	Here's an important event . . .
And another important event . . .	And another important event . . .	Here's the solution . . .	Here's what happens at the end . . .

Directors' Forms *

Directors: _____

_____	Detailed Description:	Based on These Clues:

*You can modify this general form to make it specific for each of the directors' crews. Fill in the appropriate crew name on the top line. Then fill in the left column heading with the appropriate title: "Characters Needed" (for Casting Directors); "Props Needed" (for Prop Directors); "Different Scenes Needed" (for Scenery Directors); "Costumes Needed" (for Costume Directors); "Directions Needed—One Scene" (for Stage Directors).

Beginning, Middle, End Story Map

Student: _____ Date: _____ Story Title: _____

In the Beginning	In the Middle	In the End

Main Character: _____

Setting: _____

What Happens? _____
_____
_____

Problem: _____

Main Events: _____
_____
_____

Solution: _____

Conclusion: _____
_____
_____

Text Signals Chart

Title	Headings and Subheadings	Beginning	Key Words
What do you know about this topic? Topic: _____	What do they say is important?	What big idea is shared?	Which words stand out?

Signal Words	Graphics and Captions	Graphics and Captions	Ending
Which words can you scan and spot that tell you something is important?	What do they tell you?	What do they tell you?	What big idea is shared? Compare it with the beginning big idea.

Anderson, R.C., & Pearson, P.D. (1984). A schema-theoretic view of basic processes in reading. In P.D. Pearson (Ed.), *Handbook of Reading Research*. White Plains, NY: Longman.

Bare, C. S. (1994). *Never kiss an alligator!* New York: Puffin Books.

Barrie, J. M. (2003). *Peter Pan: The original story (100th Anniversary ed.).* New York: Henry Holt and Co.

Bloom, B. (1999). *Wolf.* New York: Scholastic.

Borduin, B. J., Borduin, C. M., & Manley, C. M. (1994). The use of imagery training to improve reading comprehension of second graders. *The Journal of Genetic Psychology, 155*(1), 115–118.

Bransford, J.D., Barclay, J.R., & Franks, J.J. (1972). Sentence memory: a constructive versus interpretive approach. *Cognitive Psychology, 3*, 193-209.

Bromley, K., Irwin-De Vitis, L., & Modlo, M. (1995). *Graphic organizers: Visual strategies for active learning.* New York: Scholastic.

Bunting, E. (1989). *The Wednesday surprise.* New York: Clarion Books.

Col, J. Aall aabout aardvarks. Retrieved Dec. 2006 from Enchanted Learning: http://www.enchantedlearning.com

Col, J. All about pandas. Retrieved Dec. 2006 from Enchanted Learning: http://www.enchantedlearning.com

Cunningham, P. M., Hall, D. P., & Sigmon, C. M. (2000). *The teacher's guide to the four-blocks.* Greensboro, NC: Carson-Dellosa Publishing Company.

Dole, J.A., Duffy, G.G., Roehler, L.R. & Pearson, P.D. (1991). Moving from the old to the new: Research on reading comprehension instruction. *Review of Educational Research, 61*, 239-264.

Durkin, D. (1993). *Teaching them to read* (6th ed.). Boston: Allyn & Bacon.

Fowler, A. (1999). *Our living forests.* New York: Children's Press.

Friedrich, E. (1996). *Leah's pony.* Honesdale, PA: Boyds Mills Press.

Gambrell, L. B., & Koskinen, P. S. (2002). Imagery: A strategy for enhancing comprehension. In C. C. Block & M. Pressley (Eds.), *Comprehension instruction: Research-based best practices.* New York: Guilford Press.

Harcourt Science. (2000). How rocks change. In Harcourt Science *Earth Science Teacher's Edition, Grade 4.* Orlando, FL: Harcourt School Publishers.

Harris, T. L., & Hodges, R. E. (Eds.). (1995). *The literacy dictionary: The vocabulary of reading and writing.* Newark, DE: International Reading Association.

Harvey, S., & Goudvis, A. (2000). *Strategies that work: Teaching comprehension to enhance understanding.* Portland, ME: Stenhouse Publishers.

Hess, D. (1994). *Wilson sat alone.* New York: Simon & Schuster Children's Publishing.

Hest, A. (2004). *Mr. George Baker.* Cambridge, MA: Candlewick Press.

Homer. (2000). Cave of the one-eyed giant. In *The Odyssey.* Pollard, B. (Illus.). Denver, CO: Shortland Publications, Inc.

Hoyt, L. (1999). *Revisit, reflect, retell: Strategies for improving reading comprehension.* Portsmouth, NH: Heinemann.

Johnston, P. H., & Winograd, P. N. (1985). Passive failure in reading. *Journal of Reading Behavior , 17* (4), 279-301.

Keene, E. O., & Zimmermann, S. (1997). *Mosaic of thought: Teaching comprehension in a reader's workshop.* Portsmouth, NH: Heinemann.

BIBLIOGRAPHY

Kenah, K. (2004). *Nature's amazing partners.* Extreme readers. Columbus, OH: Waterbird Books.

Kenah, K. (2004). *Predator attack!* Extreme readers. Columbus, OH: Waterbird Books.

Kenah, K. (2004). *Tiny terrors.* Extreme readers. Columbus, OH: Waterbird Books.

Krull, K. (1992). *Gonna sing my head off!: American folk songs for children.* New York: Alfred A. Knopf, Inc.

Kurtz, J. (1998). *Fire on the mountain.* New York: Aladdin Paperbacks.

Laminack, L. (2004). *Saturdays and teacakes.* Atlanta, GA: Peachtree Publishers.

Levin, J. R., & Divine-Hawkins, P. (1974). Visual imagery as a prose-learning process. *Journal of Reading Behavior,* 6, 23–30.

Lionni, Leo. (1963). *Swimmy.* New York: Dragonfly/Knopf Books for Young Readers.

Miller, D. (2002). *Reading with meaning, teaching comprehension in the primary grades.* Portland, ME: Stenhouse Publishers.

National Reading Panel Report. (2000). Bethesda, MD: National Reading Panel.

National Institute of Child Health and Human Development. (2000). *Report of the National Reading Panel. Teaching children to read: An evidence-based assessment of the scientific research literature on reading and its implications for reading instruction* (NIH Publication No. 00-4769). Washington, DC: U.S. Government Printing Office.

Numeroff, L. J. (1985). *If you give a mouse a cookie.* New York: Laura Geringer/HarperCollins Publishers.

Numeroff, L. J. (1991). *If you give a moose a muffin.* New York: Laura Geringer/HarperCollins Publishers.

Osborne, W., & Osborne, M. P. (2001). *Pirates.* Magic tree house research guide. New York: Random House Books for Young Readers.

Osborne, W., & Osborne, M. P. (2003). *Twisters and other terrible storms.* Magic tree house research guide. New York: Random House Books for Young Readers.

Parrish, P. (1988). *Amelia Bedelia's family album.* New York: Greenwillow Books.

Pearson, P.D. & Duke, N. K. (2002). Chapter 10: Effective practices for developing reading comprehension. In *What research has to say about reading instruction* (3rd ed.). Newark, DE: International Reading Association.

Quiri, P. R. (1998). *The bald eagle.* Danbury, CT: Children's Press.

Steltzer, U. (1999). Building an igloo. *Click, 2(1),* 24–31.

Tei, E., & Stewart, O. (1985). Effective studying from text. *Forum for Reading, 16(2),* 46-55.

Tovani, C. (2000). *I read it, but I don't get it: Comprehension strategies for adolescent readers.* Portland, ME: Stenhouse Publishers.

Van Allsburg, C. (1988). *Two bad ants.* New York: Houghton Mifflin Co.

Van Steenwyk, E. (2000). *When Abraham talked to the trees.* Grand Rapids, MI: Eerdmans Books for Young Readers.

Winter, J. (2006). *Mama: A true story in which a baby hippo loses his mama during a tsunami but finds a new home, and a new mama.* Orlando, FL: Harcourt Inc.

Wood, A. (1986). *Moonflute.* Orlando, FL: Harcourt Children's Books.

Ziefert, H. (2006). Henry's wrong turn. *I'm going to read!* New York: Sterling Publishing Co.